Contents

Foreword		2
PREFACE		4
1	"THE DIAGNOSIS"	6
2	"THE FIRST NIGHT"	9
3	"THE SURGERY"	14
4	"TREATMENTS AFTER SURGERY"	18
5	"JOURNEY COMPLETED"	24
6	"THE STORY IS NOT OVER"	29
7	"COURAGE"	33
8	"LOVE OF LIFE"	38
9	"FAMILY SUPPORT"	46
10	"FAMILY STORIES"	50
11	"LOVE OF FAMILY AND SPORTS LIFE"	53
12	"HOSPITAL/CLINIC STORIES"	59
13	"MORE STORIES"	65
Photographs		72
14	"JOURNALING"	89

15	"MEMENTOS"	92
16	"THE POWER OF PRAYER"	104
17	"SAYING GOODBYE"	109
18	"ANNIVERSARY MARKERS"	120
19	"COPING WITH GRIEF"	124
20	"BLESSINGS"	134
21	"A MOTHER'S LOVE & STRENGTH"	141
22	"PURITY OF HEART"	147
23	"LINDSI'S LEGACY"	150

EPILOGUE	156
Author Biography	179

ACKNOWLEDGEMENTS

First and foremost, I want to thank God for calling me to write this book and for His inspiration. I also want to thank my former pastor, Bro. Barry Corbett, for his spiritual support, visits, and prayers for us during our time of grief and sorrow and also for writing the foreword for my book.

I also want to thank my parents for all of their love, support, and prayers. Also a word of thanks to extended family members who helped my family and me in some way. To the many others in our community and abroad, I am so thankful for their many acts of kindness and the multitude of prayers lifted toward Heaven for not only Lindsi but for my family and me.

Lastly, I give praise to my Heavenly Father for His love, mercy, and grace bestowed upon our entire family. I thank Him for His ever-present comfort and peace. All glory and honor to God above.

Foreword

Barry C. Corbett, Pastor of FBC, Kosciusko
1991-2021

We will travel many roads in our lifetime—some of which are smooth and straight, taking us to wonderful places filled with joyfulness. Other roads are adventurous, with curves, hills, and exciting sights and sounds that call us to continue our travels. Then there are roads we try to avoid due to the darkness, the storms, and the unknown, fearful destinations. On this dismal road, we endure unwanted experiences such as hurt, pain, sickness, disappointments, and the death of loved ones, which are inevitably followed by deep grief. Unfortunately, the dark road is usually a long journey, intertwined with many side roads, stops, and dangers.

As you read *Lindsi's Legacy: Her Life, Light, and Love*, you will travel with Lindsi's father, Tim, her mother, Wanda, and her brothers, Logan and Larson as they found themselves on a difficult road of darkness, fear, and grief. You will discover how Lindsi's phenomenal faith, even as a child, shined in remarkable ways. From her initial diagnosis, through her difficult days of dealing with the effects of cancer, to handling the devastation of chemotherapy, she showed spiritual strength beyond her years.

I will always treasure my visits with her, seeing her sweet smile and watching her muster the strength to speak as we prayed together for God's power. I truly witnessed the great faith of a child of God fully trusting Him with her future. Her family's steady faith in the Lord Jesus Christ was clearly evident. Never leaving nor forsaking them, God guided them throughout every step of this journey. The Lord's mighty hand and His faithful promises remained steadfast.

This road of grief is one that Tim and his family have personally traveled. His insight plus his faith in the Lord will truly prove helpful for all of us as we traverse our own roads in this ole world. One day, Jesus will return, "And God will wipe away every tear from their eyes; there shall be no more death, nor sorrow nor crying. There shall be no more pain, for the former things have passed away" (Revelation 21:4 NKJV).

Barry C. Corbett

for them speaking to God on Lindsi's behalf. I know He heard each one of them.

Finally, we received word that the surgery was over and that Lindsi was okay. They would take her back to her room at a later time. Wanda and I breathed a sigh of relief, but we were both anxious to see her again. I could barely sit still, but it would be some time before she'd be able to have visitors, so we waited. Wanda and I were emotionally exhausted and had not eaten for hours.

"Let's go to the cafeteria," Wanda said to me, with a hand on my shoulder.

Hand in hand, we made our way to the cafeteria, got some food, and sat down to eat. We had only taken a few bites when Lindsi's neurosurgeon came walking our way. He saw us and then walked over to our table.

"What's wrong? Is Lindsi okay?" I asked.

"She's fine," he answered. "I'm on my way to another appointment, so I just thought I'd say hello."

"I'm sorry," I exclaimed. "We're just on pins and needles right now."

He smiled at us and said, "I understand. You know," he continued, "I've performed countless surgeries over my many years of practice as a neurosurgeon, and I can honestly say that I believe that the resection of Lindsi's tumor is one of the best I've ever performed."

"Really?" I asked him with some surprise in my voice.

He then held his hands up. "Now, I wasn't able to remove all of the tumor. I got most of it. I went as far into her brain as I could go without causing a risk of brain damage."

His last statement quickly squelched our temporary excitement. His first declaration was a positive one and brought us sudden hope, but his second one dampened our spirits just as fast. We, of course, thanked him for his efforts and his concern for Lindsi's welfare. We also believed that he did his absolute best for our daughter, as he had told us earlier he would strive to do.

After the conversation with the doctor, Wanda and I finished our meal but remained at our table for a little while longer. We talked about what the doctor had just revealed to us and then moved on to a discussion about what lay ahead for Lindsi. We encouraged each other to stay strong for one another and for Lindsi and to remain hopeful that her treatments would shrink and eventually destroy the rest of her tumor.

Chapter 4

"TREATMENTS AFTER SURGERY"

Lindsi was eventually brought back to a private room after surgery. It would be a lengthy period before she could regain sufficient strength to be discharged from the hospital.

When that day finally arrived, I don't know if Lindsi's spirits were lifted much, even as the hospital staff wheeled her out. She was still extremely sick and weak, but as we made our way back home, I hoped she was feeling better emotionally. After all, my little girl had endured so much pain and misery during her first stint in the hospital, and I just wanted her to have some relief. I certainly think she felt some comfort after she finally got back home.

Unfortunately, Lindsi's journey would still be an exceptionally long one—and for our family as well. There would be many more steps that she would have to make in her battle with cancer.

Lindsi's next stage would involve her prescribed treatments post-op. After some time back home, she would have to travel to the Children's Cancer Clinic, which was adjoined to the Blair

Batson Children's Hospital, where Lindsi had her initial stay during her surgeries.

Wanda and I had a scheduled meeting with the assigned oncologist, who would go over the details of Lindsi's treatment plans. Because of the aggressiveness of the tumor growth, Lindsi would need to undergo both chemotherapy and radiation conjunctively.

The oncologist briefed us on all the side effects and issues that would result from these treatments. As Lindsi's parents, the information provided by the oncologist absolutely floored us. Hearing that our daughter would suffer these effects—and at such a young age—overwhelmed us. The surgeries had already traumatized her body, and she was still suffering from the tumor.

The news of the impacts of these treatments was heartbreaking. We were told that she would lose some or all of her hair. Lindsi had long, beautiful, brownish/blonde hair. She would also lose some of her hearing. In addition, she would experience difficulty in walking and would most likely be confined to a wheelchair. The thought of these projected side effects was saddening.

Still, we held onto hope that despite the serious side effects, the treatments would heal Lindsi's body and put her cancer into remission.

Lindsi began her treatments soon after this meeting. I can't recall the exact volume of required treatments that Lindsi received, but I can say there were many she had to endure. I just couldn't believe that a child would have to go through so many of them while also being given another kind of treatment at the same time. Lindsi had to make extensive trips over an hour away to receive all of them.

Initially, she handled the treatments okay, but later on, I witnessed its effects on her.

I came across some information about a medicine that was made from a substance found in nature.

Honestly, I don't recall the name of this medication, but it had been utilized in treating brain cancers. I came across studies that examined the effectiveness of this medication on the type of tumor Lindsi was diagnosed with.

I discussed my idea with Wanda, and she agreed with me. Of course, we consulted with the oncologist and other medical staff for approval before considering administering it to Lindsi. They consented to our request to pursue the use of this alternative medicine.

I chose this medicine because of the reported studies regarding its efficacy. The study indicated that there was specific evidence to look for to judge its effectiveness. I placed an order for the medication and soon started Lindsi on the scheduled regimen for its use. It was to be taken orally. Lindsi did her best to take a pill each time it was required.

After some time had elapsed, I began to see physical evidence indicated in the study I had read. At this point, I became hopeful that this alternative medicine was working at diminishing Lindsi's tumor. Lindsi's oncologist would soon schedule another MRI.

As it turned out, the tumor growth had not been slowed. This medicine may have, indeed, eradicated some of the tumor, but if so, it couldn't keep up with the pace of the tumor's rapid growth. I don't remember at what point we dispensed with the use of those pills, but I think it was shortly after Lindsi's latest MRI.

Like most, at times, we questioned God as to why He was allowing this to happen to our child. Lindsi was such a caring, loving soul, and she loved God. We didn't understand why God was allowing her pain and suffering. Instead, God wanted us to be still and realize that He is God and God alone. He is in control of everything in this life and the hereafter. There is so much more awaiting us after this life, and that is eternity with God.

We question God in our humanness as we see things in the here and now, but when we doubt God, we temporarily lose sight of His power. When Wanda and I questioned God, we failed to recognize, in that moment, that God was our strength and comfort. He was our refuge.

We live in a fallen creation because of the first sin committed by Adam and Eve, and because of this, sickness and death exist in this world, but by God's grace and mercy, He brought us His son, Jesus, to redeem us from sin and give us victory over death. We are no longer separated from God by sin. Jesus paid the price for our sins and brought us back into fellowship with God. Death was defeated, and eternal life is now available to all who accept Jesus as their personal Lord and Savior.

When those thoughts come to mind, questioning God is pointless. He is the ruler over all things—and that includes humanity. He created us, and not only that, but He also made us in His image. God has a place ready for us, as believers, when He calls us home to be with Him.

Even though we questioned our Heavenly Father, God was about to reveal to us His plan for Lindsi's life here on Earth.

Chapter 5

"JOURNEY COMPLETED"

This part of Lindsi's life story is the most painful for me to write about. Lindsi had experienced what seemed to be more pain than any small child should have to bear. Her body had been prodded with needles countless times, and she was required to travel extensively in her sickened condition and deprived of sleep. And yet, she rarely complained about any of it. She had traveled down a long road, but she fought her sickness with amazing strength and resilience. Her bravery was awe-inspiring.

One day, we were asked if we could meet with a group of doctors for a consultation. We confirmed our availability and scheduled a meeting shortly after that. As we approached the meeting venue, several doctors were seated at a table in a small room. Wanda and I walked in and sat down across the table from them. At this juncture, we were extremely exhausted—both mentally and physically. We had spent days and weeks at a time in the hospital to be there for Lindsi.

Lindsi was hospitalized when this meeting took place. For me, this meeting was frightening, and I'm sure it was for

Wanda. They got right to the point and were forthright in their words to us.

"All our efforts at this point have been unsuccessful in destroying Lindsi's tumor," one doctor remarked.

Another doctor spoke up and told us, "Unfortunately, there is nothing else we can do for Lindsi, so she will be discharged from the hospital as soon as she feels strong enough to go home."

These were not the conclusions we wanted to hear. And then, the devastating news was delivered.

"Lindsi will not have much longer to live, so we recommend she receive hospice care upon her return home."

After being told this, Wanda and I fell into instant despair. We sat there in utter sorrow.

Following this tragic news, we were given even more horrifying information. The doctors laid out the phases that Lindsi would go through before her death. Then, they concluded the meeting by telling us to make things as comfortable as possible for Lindsi.

I have an admission to make. After processing all the terrible news given to us by these doctors, I viewed each of them as uncaring and unthoughtful. They just sat there, calmly in their chairs, after telling us that our daughter would not be on this Earth much longer. To me, they seemed to show very little sympathy or remorse toward us. Those were my initial feelings toward them, but later, I thought back on my reactions and considered things from their perspectives as doctors. I think most doctors try to distance themselves emotionally from the patient and their families, but deep down, they experience distress—especially when they can no longer do anything for a terminally ill one. I also considered that these doctors likely had meetings like ours daily. So, I tried to put myself in their shoes and look at this from their viewpoint.

After that fateful meeting, Wanda and I had to compose ourselves, yet again, and be strong for Lindsi—and to hold back tears before going back to her room. That was so incredibly difficult to do, especially when Lindsi wanted to know what was going to happen next. This would be the beginning of the end of Lindsi's earthly journey—and our last stage as her caregivers.

It hurt so much because we knew we were going to lose our sweet Lindsi. However, God empowered us to stay strong, and we poured out our enormous love for her. We had prayed for a miracle to be performed by God through the doctors, but that miracle never came.

Thinking back, I'm so thankful that Wanda and I were saved. Both of us had accepted Christ very early in our lives. With knowing and accepting Jesus, each of us still had hope, even amid knowing that we would lose our precious daughter. In that hope, we still had faith that if God so chose, He could and would still perform a miracle. God had prepared both of us for this time in our lives. He was going to make a way for us to cope with the impending death of our child.

Lindsi would later build up enough strength to be discharged from the hospital. After we returned home, Lindsi would be bedridden. She had spent months and months in bed throughout her sickness, and sometimes, she asked to be moved around in bed to give her some momentary comfort. She asked so many times to be repositioned. It was so sad to see her confined to a bed for hours and days at a time. She was in such a helpless state, and I wanted so much to be able to take her pain away. Often, I would ask God to ease her pain.

The remainder of this chapter is very difficult for me to share. As I revisit this moment back in time, the anguish, grief, and sadness resurfaces.

One night, Lindsi began moaning constantly. She was very uncomfortable and wanted to be moved to another bed in the house. She was in our master bedroom bed at the time. During this time, we were told not to move her, as doing so would be very dangerous. But her cries became louder and louder. Then she started begging and pleading to be moved. As I stood there, my heart grievously ached for Lindsi. She was in so much discomfort and pain.

Then she looked up at me and said, "Daddy, please."

Her plea pierced my heart, and I could not deny her request any longer. So, I reached down and cradled her frail body in my arms, and as I carried her to the other room, she cried out in agony. I was in tears because I knew it would be the last time I could do this for her. I moved her to the bedroom directly across the hall from the master bedroom—the room where Lindsi would take her last breath.

Wanda and I lay beside Lindsi on that bed, one on each side. All we could do now was hold her and talk to her. Wanda and I kept telling Lindsi over and over that we loved her. As Wanda and I held Lindsi, I wondered when the moment would come—when Lindsi would take her final breath. Eventually, her breathing slowed, and then we could barely hear a breath, and then, we heard it no more.

Lindsi's eyes were still open, and I remember lifting my hand to her face and gently closing her eyes. As I removed my hand from them, one eye remained open. I felt as if she was trying to hold on and not leave us just yet. Maybe God was allowing Lindsi to look at us one last time.

As I wrote this, tears were rolling down my face. And each time I reflect on that moment, my weeping returns. Oh, I miss her so. That day, Lindsi left us to go to her eternal home in Heaven. She was released from all of her sickness and pain. Our farewell will one day become a reunion, and that is such a comforting thought that is only made possible through God's love for us.

I offered a synopsis of Lindsi's journey battling cancer to begin the book—a very dark time for all the family. Lindsi had lived a remarkable life before and after she was stricken with cancer. Now, I want to turn away from this dark period and share about other times in Lindsi's life—good stories about my wonderful daughter and the the happiness she brought to us in our lives.

I hope these remembrances will encourage you and that you will see the importance of recognizing God's power and love in the best and worst of times. Whatever you may go through, know that God cares for you. He cares for every one of us. As you continue reading, you will see God's work through Lindsi's life—and the lives of others.

The story of Lindsi's life is not over. There are many more accounts to share. Lindsi's legacy keeps her story alive to this day.

Chapter 6

"THE STORY IS NOT OVER"

So far, you have read about a dire period we experienced as a family. It was a time of great unrest and sadness. We had ventured into the unknown, but God had mapped out our steps before we took them. God met Lindsi and us at our point of need and gave us the strength to plant our feet onto the ground to withstand the onslaught of challenges that awaited us. Lindsi's life had been shaken to the core, along with ours, but her story was not over after her sickness. It continues to this day. I feel blessed that I can share her life story.

People often posed common questions about hope during our life struggles.

"Where is hope found in a person who is lost?"

"How can they find any hope at all?"

I have asked myself these questions and given it some thought. One inference that came to mind was that if a lost person's hope is not in God, then he or she will most likely search for it in the wrong places or wrong things, and that will never turn out well. These "wrong" places or things might bring some consolation, but they will only be temporary, and they will become folly for those who seek escape from their pain.

Surrendering to God and leaning on Him is the only hope we have, and He is there for us if we call upon His name.

As stated earlier, Wanda and I accepted Christ at an early age. We knew where our hope was found. Our prayers for Lindsi's physical healing were not answered, but God never walked away from us. Instead, He lifted us up to continue moving forward in life, and His footprints were right there alongside ours as we traveled on through this journey. The trek was dark, but God lit our path along the way.

So much has taken place since I began writing this book. Many years have passed by and, with it, both joy and sorrow. I still experience the grief of losing Lindsi, and the pain still lingers, but I press on each day with a thankful heart for the time I had with her. You know, most of us rarely or maybe never think that we will outlive our children, but death will eventually come for all of us. Lindsi's death shook me to my core, but I knew in my heart that I could not stop in my tracks and fall into a sea of deep depression.

Sometimes, God will allow difficulties in our lives to strengthen our faith in Him and to cause us to realize our dependence on Him. We need God all the time.

I've heard it said that God will stretch our faith. Hard times may come at us in waves, and they may stick around for long periods. In this way, God is elongating our faith, as it requires us to trust Him more and to exert patience to wait on Him.

Lindsi's trial in life was a lengthy one, as it was for us. Our faith was being stretched through Lindsi's long battle with cancer. God picked our family up and carried us along the extensive path of our trial in life. Several years later, we would need to be picked up yet again.

Wanda, my wonderful wife of nearly twenty-five years, passed away. She died from Covid-19, the deadly virus that was leaked out of a lab in China. This outbreak brought grief and heartache to many other families. Wanda passed away in 2021, just over nine years after Lindsi's death. She was just fifty-one years old. She was healthy and had no underlying medical conditions. We are a family of three now, rather than five. I'm now a widower with two sons who have lost their mother and sister.

Understand that the central theme of the book is about my daughter, but many things can transpire over a period of ten years. I will have much more to say about my wife later. When Wanda died, we once again had our faith stretched. Our family dynamic might look helpless to those of you reading this book, but it isn't. I'm grateful that I still have my two sons with me, and I often tell others that through all this pain in life, God also blessed us. I share this with others because I want them to know that God is still God, and He is always there to meet us with our greatest and smallest needs.

At the outset, this book was conceived to share the story of Lindsi through the eyes of her father. I felt led by God to pursue writing a testimony about her life. At that time, I never expected that this book would also include a story about losing my wife.

My situation now, and that of my family, is not an uncommon one. Many people encounter tests and trials in their lives. It is my prayer, through this book, that you will find encouragement and strength when times of trials come your way. More importantly, I want God to be magnified and exalted. I also hope, if it is His will, that it might touch the hearts and minds of both the saved and unsaved. May His will be done.

Lindsi's story is not over. There is so much more to share with you. As I put all of my sporadic writings together for the manuscript, I decided to first cover the timeline of Lindsi's sickness. This timeline would be focused mainly on her onset of symptoms up to her passing.

Now, I want to tell you more about Lindsi, my family, and many other stories. I mentioned earlier that there would be stories of positivity to share going forward, but I did not include the caveat of a few more sad ones to be interspersed as well. But through these recollections, you will see the power of God and His daily presence in our lives.

Chapter 7

"COURAGE"

Again, I just can't imagine the emotions that Lindsi experienced from the time she was diagnosed. She was in so much pain and rarely had good days. It just broke our hearts to see her suffering. She dealt with so many physical issues, and her struggles were mighty. Those feelings of helplessness took hold of me so many times, as I know it must have for Wanda.

As a parent, you want the ability to take away your child's pain and suffering—or at least have the capability to minimize it. Great care had to be taken whenever Lindsi needed to be moved for anything. Once she was permanently confined to a bed, she found it extremely difficult because she could only remain in a position for brief moments at a time. She could not find positions on the bed to give her any long periods of comfort. She would constantly cry out that she needed to be repositioned. It was just awful to witness her current physical state of being. We strove to not allow Lindsi to see how much we were hurting inwardly for her. We needed to be both positive and supportive toward her and to make absolutely every effort possible to assist her and meet her constant needs.

Lindsi knew she had a brain tumor, and, at some point, I think she knew her earthly life would end, but I can tell you she fought her cancer until the very end. The courage shown by our little girl was beyond belief. She fought it for about a year and a half, and though she knew her sickness was a serious one, she did not give up, even in light of her terminal condition. Lindsi had only been on Earth for what seemed a very brief moment, but her resolve was akin to that of an older, mature adult. She was what some people might term an "old soul." Her qualities mirrored those of a loving and caring adult. Rather, it was as if she was a grown-up living in the body of a little girl.

"How was it possible for our small child to exemplify these characteristics?" I think I have a plausible answer. I believe Lindsi's wonderful traits can only be explained by her deep, personal relationship with God.

Lindsi was very active in church. She sang in the children's choir and also took part in our church programs. She was a happy person most of the time, and she would show her beautiful smile often. Lindsi had not yet made a public profession of faith, but I know she had a strong, spiritual relationship with God, regardless. I believe her actions and deeds reflected that relationship and her love for God. I also feel that she was willing to serve Him as a vessel to carry out His plans and that she was following in the footsteps of His will for her.

God can use those who are willing to serve Him and to be used in such a way as to give God radiant glory. I can't think of any other reasonable explanations as proof of how Lindsi lived her life or the endearing qualities that she possessed. Besides her remarkable courage, Lindsi exuded inward strength and a loving, caring disposition.

God opened up my eyes to these traits as I witnessed her life. It caused me to pause and take an inventory of how I was living my own life from day to day and in what areas I needed to make improvements. It impressed upon me that we, as believers, are to make efforts to meet the needs of others. We may not always be successful in doing that, but we should make it a priority to do so. We don't have to look very far to find needs. These needs might be prevalent within our own family, extended family, or even our next-door neighbors. There are needs all around us, and God desires for each of us to meet the needs of humankind. We show our love for Him by loving and helping other people.

Lindsi made an impression on me in this way, and I have been told that she touched the lives of others as well. As Christians, we should be willing servants of God. Lindsi demonstrated this as she lived a life that was pleasing to God. She had a genuine concern for others, loved people, and desired to help them, which brought joy into people's lives. She placed others before herself and served them. Helping and caring for humanity should be an outward extension of our love for God, and when we do this in a genuine, loving, and willing way, we honor God, and it is pleasing to Him. Lindsi honored God in her brief life. Part of her epitaph reads: "A loving and caring heart. A shining light for God and a powerful legacy left for Him."

Looking back at our family adventure through a dark labyrinth of the unknown with Lindsi's cancer, I recall the light that God provided for our pathway. The other light He provided was the one that emanated from our daughter. God dispelled the darkness of our journey with His manifold provisions. He provided illumination for us to move forward in the darkness of our travels through His mercy and grace. Through it, we witnessed His power, majesty, and sovereignty. Lindsi shined her light for God by bringing recognition to Him for His omnipotence and work in her life and ours. It brought glory to Him.

So often, we fail to take notice of God's goodness poured out on us. We are so fixated on trying to solve our own problems and never give thought to leaning on Him to help us. We are not promised only times without hardships in life, as they will eventually come, nor are we promised another moment of life.

Everyone will experience times of sadness, grief, and loss, but we should praise God even in those times. I understand that, as human beings, it can be challenging for us to do this, but even in those trying times, we can still experience God's love and feel His presence, as He showers us with His mercy and grace. We are to recognize Him and praise Him in our struggles as well. God is still there for us when we walk through our valleys in life.

In our family trial, we received God's bountiful blessings. These blessings were evident even through the hardships. Again, God never left our side. He was in complete control, and He was always available to us. God is immovable and always there to listen to us, especially in times of despair. We need to humble ourselves before Him, call out to Him, and make our petitions known, even though He knows them before we utter them from our mouths.

We offered many prayers to God, expressing gratitude for any fragments of good news we received. We prayed fervently for God to do a miracle of healing, but we never dismissed the reality that God's will would be done. Yes, there were those times when I did question God, but in my innermost being, I knew it would be His decision, not mine, and His will would be carried out.

Lindsi was so courageous as she faced her cancer. She was the one that was suffering, not us. And yet, she dealt with all the pain, needles, transfusions, hospital stays, chemo, radiation, sickness, etc. yet never gave up in her fight. I never once heard Lindsi complain to God or question Him about her condition. She displayed such resilience in the face of insurmountable odds. She was an incredible human being. She was a wonderful blessing to me and my family as she was to many people. Lindsi touched lives when she was healthy, when she developed cancer, and when she left this world. She left her mark on this Earth as a faithful follower of God.

I was often reminded of His love during this time. Watching Lindsi suffer was gut-wrenching. When all hope was gone, we wanted her pain and struggle to end and for her to go to her new home in Heaven, where all of that pain and suffering would cease— the place where she would receive perfect peace for eternity.

Chapter 8

"LOVE OF LIFE"

Lindsi really enjoyed life. She was content and happy most of the time. I don't recall Lindsi being hard to please or being someone to always be wanting something. Mostly, she was a compliant child at home, school, and out in public.

I was recently thumbing through a journal of mine that I've had for several years. This journal is specifically for fathers. This book contains many partially blanked pages with inscriptions at the top, directing fathers to write responses related to them. Fathers can share their memories and thoughts on the various topics offered on the pages. It also allows fathers to record any advice they would like to pass on to their children. I have made quite a few entries in my book over the years. This is not a "diary" in the traditional sense, as it is not a daily journal.

Anyway, as I was perusing it, I paused at a particular story I had written about our family, but more specifically about our children. This story involved a family night out at a restaurant. During the meal, an older woman approached our table and imparted to us that she had been observing us from a nearby table. She told Wanda and me she just wanted to come over and let us know we had the most well-behaved children. This meant so much to both of us. We tried to instill Christian values in our children very early in their lives. I'm uncertain, but I think Larson had not been born yet. For us, as parents, this was a great example and reminder that, sometimes, others are watching, especially those who may know you personally. This woman, however, didn't know us, nor did we know her, but she was paying attention to our family that night.

We may not always think about being under the observation or scrutiny of other people or even aware of it, but there may be someone, somewhere, with their eyes on us—watching to see how we conduct ourselves. Those times may include those when we are reacting to a tense or delicate situation. We, as Christians, are under the human microscope, and the viewers might just be unbelievers. They may be curious to discover if we will stumble in our walk with God in different situations.

One thing is for certain—God is always watching us. He observed Lindsi's life on this Earth, and I believe that what He witnessed of her gave Him joy. She loved God, and her life was a testament to her love for Him. She not only talked the talk, but she walked in her faith and love for God.

Not only did Lindsi enjoy life itself, but she also enjoyed living her life. Before the diagnosis, she was a very active child. She enjoyed playing softball and basketball, but I think her favorite thing to do was cheer gymnastics. She appeared to love cheering in front of a large audience. Lindsi was a member of a local gymnastics group in our hometown called the Mid-South Extreme. It was a large organization with different age groups that competed in and out of state. She really seemed to enjoy it. Physically, Lindsi was very strong. In the routines where they would form a pyramid, Lindsi would be one of the team members who would stand on the floor and be the anchor and hoist another girl up on her shoulders or hold her up with her hands.

I wonder, at times, if she would have stayed with gymnastics or any of the other sports she played if she was still with us and if she would have considered being a cheerleader in her junior high and high school years.

If you have ever attended a cheer/gymnastics competition, you know how long they can last. You could count on it being a full day because of the excessive number of teams entered. This group traveled long distances and competed in big venues. One thing I remember about those events was the noise. The music played was so loud, and the waiting periods to see Lindsi and the team perform were very long.

Wanda and I tried to be at every event, game, or church program that our children were involved in. If one of us was unavailable to go, then the other would usually be present. There were also those times when two children would have something on the same day, so we had to decide where I was going and where Wanda would go. For me, working out of town and so far from home was sometimes problematic. Yes, it was very tiring, but we wanted to be there to show them our support and cheer them on.

I have so many wonderful memories over the years, celebrating championships and many wins, but I also have fond memories even in the losses. Spending time together as a family is so important. Our years as parents to three wonderful children passed by so quickly. At the time of writing this, my oldest son, Logan, is now twenty- four years old. He's engaged to be married later this year. My youngest son, Larson, is now nineteen and attending college. He is already a junior, as he completed some college credits while in high school and attending summer school this year. Lindsi would have been twenty-two now.

It was a joy to watch Lindsi play sports and sing in the choir. You could see her joy in doing them. Her precious smile confirmed it, and she enjoyed her life. I think I can say that she did up until her sickness, but she still tried to be happy in her dire situation, and I admired her so much for the way she handled the cancer that would later take her from us. Her life was shortened, but despite the brevity of it, I still cherish it. She brought so much elation and inspiration into our lives.

We were so humbled to be chosen as her parents and thankful for the time we had with her in this life. I know Lindsi is, without a doubt, now a cheerleader in Heaven, praising God. There has to be cheering there because everyone is praising God forevermore. In faith, I believe that Lindsi, and now her mother, are one of the many who are singing and shouting praises to God for eternity.

Cherish those moments with your children. Make the most of the fleeting time that they are in your care. Do not take this time for granted. Make every effort to be there for them and to give them support. I don't mean support only for sports or other events of your children, but also for emotional, moral, and spiritual support. Today's generation deals with so many pressures. In our present society, Satan constantly bombards children and adults alike with so many temptations.

God wants us to walk the straight and narrow road and to be a positive influence in our children's lives. He wants us to train them in His ways, and hopefully, when they mature into adulthood, they will not turn away from those teachings. I know that there may be other things that might come into play, causing a parent's absence, but every opportunity to be there for your child or children is vital. We also need to pray for our children daily.

Your children need you and your presence, whether it be at a church, gymnasium, ball field, or at home. Children need guidance. They need a moral compass. They can easily take the wrong path in life, and once they choose that path, it can be a long road back to rediscovering the right one.

Be accountable to your children. God did not give you a child to wander aimlessly in this world. Children are a blessing from God. The birth of a child is a miracle of God. Seek God for guidance and wisdom in parenting your children. Being a parent can be a challenge, but God provides the means to raise a child. We should all look to Him for wisdom to give us guidance for parenting because He instructs us to instill His words in our children. Difficult times may surface in parenthood, but God is always there to lend us His guiding hands. We only need to call upon His name and ask for it. We should acknowledge His power and ask for His direction in humility. God will supply our needs and guide us with His Holy Spirit. Again, our children need us, but more importantly, they need God.

Lindsi had an unforgettable smile. Her happy countenance could brighten one's day. I think it was one of her characteristic traits I most remember about her and also her loving-kindness. Even those memories of the smiles she would muster through all of her pain and sickness remain. As I remarked earlier, Lindsi was such an inspiration to our family, but she also inspired other people in her life, those she met for the first time after she became ill, and even those who followed her battle that never met her. I cannot overstate her courage and strength.

I become heartbroken every time I see a public service announcement or a story about children with cancer. This really hits home for me and instantly affects me every time. I have seen and experienced the impact of cancer and its ripple effects on the whole family. As soon as I see one of those spots, I immediately shut the tv off or change the channel. If I were to hear one on the radio, I'm sure my reaction would be the same. Childhood cancers are so prevalent, and there are many forms of it. I wish we could eradicate all cancers, but again, we live in a fallen world, and sickness will continue to exist in this life. Hopefully, we can find cures to combat at least some of these cancers.

There were so many children that we encountered at the clinic. Lindsi had many appointments there, so we were there often. Some patients suffered from leukemia, and then others, like Lindsi, had tumors. There was so much somberness in that waiting room. However, groups of people stationed inside the clinic sought to bring the children fun and a little joy during the appointment waits.

At one of Lindsi's visits, an artist was there. He offered to draw caricatures of patients. He would also ask each child how he/she would like to be drawn. For instance, the artist could draw them as a princess or a baseball player. The choice was theirs. I thought this was so great, and I really appreciated Him taking the time out of his schedule to do these drawings of the children there. He used his talent to make the visit better for each child and their families. I still have the drawings he did for each of my children.

All the other volunteers at the clinic are to be commended as well. They, too, brought some happiness in the face of sadness that engulfed that waiting room. Their efforts did not go unnoticed. I like to think that Lindsi's smile helped someone at the clinic each time she was there. If not for a fellow patient, I firmly believe that Lindsi did so for the nurses there. In fact, they frequently told us they always looked forward to Lindsi's smile whenever they found out she was scheduled to come in. I know her smile lifted me up so many times.

Occasionally, I would be so down but prayerful that Lindsi would have a good day and feel better. When her smiles were absent, I knew her day would not be a good one. I wanted to make her smile or get her to laugh about something each day. If I could see that smile again, it made me feel better.

These things may sound so simple, but seeing her smile gave me elation. Just for her to have a better day was my hope. The MRIs did not indicate healing, so just to see her have a day with less pain made my pain lessen. Lindsi did not have a smile every day. She would have more bad days than good ones, especially when she had to return to the hospital. Eventually, any reduction in her pain was all we could hope for as her cancer worsened. Wanda and I tried to make her as comfortable as possible. We desperately wanted to see glimpses of smiles from her.

After Lindsi passed on, I thought about ordering some small smiley face stickers. My plan was to affix these stickers somewhere on my clothing each day. This would be something I could do in her memory. Well, I decided against this because these stickers don't stick well on clothing, but I still have those smiley face stickers. Sometimes, I come across them, and I suddenly think of Lindsi. I think about that wide, beautiful smile of hers. I even made a smiley face refrigerator magnet from the wood of a cedar tree, and I have displayed it in the kitchen. We also had three items etched near the top of Lindsi's headstone—a peace sign, a butterfly, and, you guessed it, a smiley face.

A memory is all that I have of her now in this life, along with pictures and family movies, and I'm thankful for that. I'm also thankful that when I have passed from this earth, a blessed reunion awaits us in Heaven.

Earlier, I referred to cancer spots on tv and my reactions to them. If you watch tv much or even occasionally, you will probably run across an infomercial about childhood cancer. They are so heart-wrenching for me now. It rapidly brings back all the sorrow I experienced as a father of a sick child. I know the pain the parents are going through.

Tears quickly well up at the sight of the sick children. The presence of cancer encircles many families, regardless of the outcomes. And for those with positive outcomes, the risk for cancer to return lingers. In either situation, good or bad, it has already taken its toll on the entire family.

Again, I quickly change the channel if a cancer ad appears. A picture of a child with cancer has an identical impact on me. My emotions will change dramatically. Those painful memories are still fresh and etched in my mind. It is a struggle to block out the sadness and hurt, even after all these years. The images of cancer-stricken children trigger those thoughts of Lindsi's sickened state, so I, again, choose to turn the channel each time to deflect those remembrances.

Even though I turn away from those images, my heart aches for those sweet children and their families, along with my pain for Lindsi's suffering and my grief over her death but praise God, He provides me with peace through my sorrow, and each day, He renews it in me through the Holy Spirit. He lightened the load our family was carrying during Lindsi's illness. His promises are true, and His righteousness is forever. He is faithful to us and will never abandon us, no matter our situation. He will hold us in His hands and show us His mercy and grace. My family and I were the recipients of all these things.

My sadness is constantly being replaced by God's peace and comfort. I ask Him for it often, and He always supplies it. I can take rest, through faith, that God will continue to hear my prayers and answer them, not always in my desired ways, but His. He knows what is best for us, and His love endures forever.

God gave Lindsi a wonderful and beautiful smile. Her smile still resonates, and it reminds me that whatever I may face in life, I don't have to face it alone. Her smile reflected her contentment in this life and, later, in her battle with cancer. She committed herself to live for God and serve Him. The first sentence in Lindsi's epitaph mentions her beautiful smile. Lindsi now has that smile with her in Heaven.

Chapter 9

"FAMILY SUPPORT"

I think support from other family members is a must for the immediate family being affected by cancer. We considered ourselves blessed to have this support during Lindsi's sickness.

As I noted earlier, Wanda and I were Lindsi's primary caregivers. Caregivers need support as well. Many extended family members stepped into a role of support for us. Sometimes, we just needed to step out for some fresh air or to have a moment to eat a meal. During those times, a family member would be there to lend a hand and sit with Lindsi.

Lindsi's needs were constant, and sometimes, she would specifically want Wanda or me for something. It was a relief to have another person there to give us a temporary break so that we could have some time to take care of ourselves. We needed this in order to be there for Lindsi as often as possible.

Lindsi needed care nearly twenty-four hours and seven days a week. It was a blessing if Lindsi could sleep for an hour or two at a time. We tried to keep Lindsi at home as much as we could. This was her desire as well, but the treatments she was receiving made her prone to infections. Again, her red and white blood cell counts needed to remain high to help her avoid the threat of infections developing in her body. So, Lindsi's blood counts had to be monitored daily.

Throughout her illness, she would have many blood transfusions, as noted earlier, plus additional stays in the hospital. Other family members assisted us in a lot of ways, and they made it possible for Wanda and me to reset and enable us to be ready to return to being the support bridge that Lindsi needed—and to provide her aid for more comfort.

I have such wonderful parents, and they have been amazing grandparents to my children, who are now fully grown. They have always been very supportive of my family and my brother's family. Back during Lindsi's illness, they were always willing to help when we needed them. They opened their home to us many times throughout the years. I love them both very much. Both of them are so loving and kind-hearted. When our children were younger, they would spend quite a bit of time with them, especially when they were out of school for the summer, but as they got older and became busier with other things like sports, their visits to them dwindled. My parents live less than twenty miles from our home. They always had fun times with them on visits.

I also want to mention Wanda's parents, as they provided us with so much support and helped us out in many ways. They lived even closer to us than my parents, and they were a blessing to our family. Wanda's side of the family was larger than mine. I have one sibling, and Wanda had three.

As you can see, we had a large support base, and most everyone lived in fairly close proximity to us. This was yet another blessing from God. Our extended family members were so gracious and loving toward us. They provided us with much-needed assistance in our journey.

I enjoy listening to the stories my parents share about Lindsi. Hearing them is particularly important to me, and I'm glad they have stories to share with me. They have never shared a bad story about her, as Lindsi was a sweet girl and not mischievous. Maybe I will be told some unknown stories in the future about my precious Lindsi.

We need to hold on to the sweet stories and memories of our lost loved ones. I think it can somehow reconnect us with them, and it helps us to get past some of those times of grief and sadness. We don't need to allow our grief to take hold of us. Instead, we need to call out to God and ask for His comfort and strength to minimize our sorrow. Positive memories of loved ones are the thoughts we need to hold captive.

You've heard it said that you will find out who a true friend is when you go through tough times in life. Well, we were so blessed by the generosity of many friends and people that we didn't know at all. Their kindness and giving were overwhelming and very humbling. Many people visited Lindsi at the hospital and at home. There were so many acts of kindness shown toward Lindsi and us during the time of her cancer and after her death. Members of churches from around the area of the hospital made frequent visits and brought Lindsi gifts.

It was amazing to see God's love displayed through others, and it was in action the entire time of her sickness. It was evident that Lindsi was impacting lives, and many validated this in the words spoken to us. God can do great things through those who are willing to be used by Him. The people we encountered reflected God working through those with a willing heart to serve Him by serving others. God used these wonderful believers in a mighty way. They made our journey a little less difficult.

God can use those who believe in Him. I'm thankful to God for all those we met, whether through a visit, a kind letter, a monetary donation, an offer to help in some way, or the provision of food or prayer. The outpouring of love was incredible. Not only did Lindsi see concern from our hometown and county, but also across the state of Mississippi. It continued into other states like Florida, Iowa, and Texas. Lindsi also received prayers from a group of women in the country of Kenya. It was amazing to behold. It just speaks to the power of God and how the life of a small girl from a small city in Mississippi can impact His kingdom. God specially used these folks, and hopefully, their efforts changed lives.

After losing Lindsi, several have given donations to various organizations in her memory over the years. I appreciate, first, their willingness to give to others and, second, their remembrance of my daughter. This is yet another blessing and testament to Lindsi's life. She touched the hearts of others through not only her battle with cancer but the life she lived on this Earth.

Lindsi loved people, and she had the heart of a servant. Before she was diagnosed, she was doing work for the kingdom of God. I believe people took notice of this, and I also believe that these donations attested to the way Lindsi conducted herself. They saw her loving-kindness toward her fellow man and her eagerness to help and please others. This may have left indelible impressions on others. She pleased God with her actions. Those donations offered with willing hearts, whether made in Lindsi's memory or not, please God, too. I'm thankful for their faithfulness to give those donations.

The Bible tells us in 1st Corinthians that three things remain and this is faith, hope, and love, with the greatest of them being love (1 Cor. 13:13). Lindsi lived out all three of these in her life.

God desires the same of us.

Chapter 10

"FAMILY STORIES"

Hearing stories shared by others about Lindsi brings me joy. It centers my thoughts on her life before the sickness. Lindsi had a heart of gold. She had no filter when it came to the ages of people. She loved any and all ages. Her goodness reached out to all she encountered. Her light shined for her Lord and Savior to young and old alike.

My mom told me one story about Lindsi several years ago. One day, my mom was contemplating what to cook for a meal. Finally, she decided she would fry some okra to serve as one side for the meal. Later, she began removing the okra from the pan onto a plate for serving. As she placed the okra on the plate, Lindsi would pick one up and eat it. As it turned out, she really liked the taste of okra. She had never eaten it before. My mom then told Lindsi that she was eating the okra about as fast as she could put them on the plate. She then said that Lindsi replied, "Oh, Maw Maw."

Another time, my mom, dad, and Lindsi sat down to a meal together. My mom had prepared spaghetti on this occasion. My dad doesn't really like spaghetti. He is a picky eater, so to help this food item better suit his taste, he added some additional ingredients. I don't know what particular extras he used, but he likes to put hot sauce or pepper sauce on his food. Anyway, Lindsi asked him if she could take a bite of his spaghetti after He had doused it with other stuff. He told her it would be fine. She then took a bite and liked it.

Then, my mom said that Lindsi wanted a bite of her spaghetti and then wanted another bite from my dad's plate. My mom said that she and my dad got so tickled at Lindsi going back and forth for bites. I assume she had finished her plate before asking to have some of their food or finished up her plate later.

My dad had a story to share, too, and he has told it to me on more than one occasion. He said that Lindsi came to him and sat on his lap. Lindsi was facing my dad in this story. Lindsi leaned her body back and then extended her head all the way back and down to the floor as he held her legs. She then raised herself back up with no help, other than him still holding her knees. He has told me often how incredible that was to him, as he had never seen a child that strong. He still talks about it to this day and how it amazed him.

Now, I want to relay a beautiful story, and this one is another from my mother. She said that Lindsi and she made a trip one day to visit her mother, who was Lindsi's great-grandmother. At this time, my grandmother was well into her nineties and could not do much for herself. They arrived, and made their way into the house. My mom then said that Lindsi walked over to my grandmother, sat down beside her, took her hand, and held it about the entire time of their visit. This story was gripping.

Most children, at this young age, would be busily playing inside or outside on a visit, but not Lindsi. She was concerned about her great-grandmother. Lindsi sensed a need in her, and she made sure that she could help her in some way. It made me so proud and honored to be the father of this incredible child. I can only imagine the joy it brought to God above.

What a testimony from a little girl. We often see needs around us and do nothing. It's easy to shrug it off and make an excuse for it. We often become so engrossed in our own problems and self-centeredness that it causes us to overlook an opportunity to help someone else in need. In these moments, we should harken back to what God did for us when He gave us His son, Jesus, to be crucified for our sins. We didn't deserve to be forgiven, but, yet, Christ still died for us. God places opportunities out there before us, but so often, we turn the other way.

God opened up these times in the life of my daughter, and she answered His call to be a willing vessel for servanthood. She had so much love in her heart for other people. She wanted to be a light in this cruel, dark world. I also believe, in my heart, that Lindsi expected nothing in return, but only to serve God and to serve others. She strived to be the salt and light that He wants each of us to be—and to glorify Him. It pleases Him to see His sheep show love to others and to help those in need.

I could see this love in Lindsi in how she treated others. She was one of God's lights in this world.

Chapter 11

"LOVE OF FAMILY AND SPORTS LIFE"

I am blessed to still have two wonderful children after the losses of Lindsi and Wanda. At the time of writing this, my oldest, Logan, has already graduated from college with a degree in business administration and has moved away, but still lives about an hour away. My youngest, Larson, recently graduated high school in 2023, and as I mentioned earlier, will soon enter his junior year in college. Both of them completed a lot of college credit while in high school. Lindsi was our middle child. She was one of her brothers' biggest fans, lending her support to them in all of their sports endeavors when she was not playing a sport herself. She also cheered them on, even after her diagnosis.

Lindsi loved her brothers, and you could see it in the way she treated them. Lindsi was like a mother hen around them. She would take on a motherly persona with them if she detected misbehavior. She would also play the role of babysitter, especially if their mother wasn't present. This further illustrates her caring heart for others.

Logan and Larson loved their sister, too. Logan, being the oldest, was very protective of Lindsi. Both of our sons were very supportive of Lindsi. Larson was still a small child at the time of Lindsi's illness. He would have been five or six years old at that time. They did not exhibit any selfishness regarding the constant attention required for their sister, so Wanda and I and other family members were not Lindsi's only support group. Logan and Larson were very important supporters as well. Just thinking back on their actions brings back the pride they give me being their dad. I'm so thankful for them. All our children brought us so much contentment as well as laughter. They filled our hearts with overflowing joy.

Again, this book primarily centers on Lindsi, but I also wanted the readers to know more about the rest of our family, so forgive me for jumping back and forth. You are aware of my obvious pride in my daughter, but I'm equally proud of my two sons. They have shown incredible strength through all these years without their sweet sister, followed by the loss of their wonderful mother. Logan and Lindsi were born less than three years apart, and Larson was born a little over three years after Lindsi's birth. Logan, of course, remembers Lindsi more vividly than Larson. All of them seemed to get along, mostly.

I have a picture of the three of them after Lindsi became ill. It is the sweetest photo. Lindsi had started her treatments and had lost some of her hair. The smiles on each of their faces were priceless. They were all lying on our bed, and each one had a lollipop in their mouth. They spent a lot of time together in that room, and I believe they all cherished that time together. That picture, for me, indicated their love and concern for Lindsi.

Now, I want to share more with you about my boys. Again, they have been mighty oaks of strength in dealing with their grief and loss. They have moved on with their lives as I have, and we know this is the expectation of both Lindsi and Wanda, now in Heaven. We also realize that God desires this of us as well. After Wanda's death, I suddenly became a widower and a single parent. It has been difficult, but I can attest to the work of God in my life. He has given me the strength to overcome the obstacles in my path, and He has also filled me with a calm spirit of peace and comfort.

My sons and I have a great relationship, and we have moved on to the next stages of our lives with the support of each other and our faith in God. I often think about Lindsi and Wanda daily and their eternity in Heaven now. In my human selfishness, I want them back here with me again, but when I come back to the realization of the eternal, big picture, I rejoice in their salvation and our eternal reunion one day. That thought brings me the comfort and peace of God.

Logan and Larson have accepted Jesus and have been baptized. I am so thankful for our salvation and that all of us will be together again in eternity. If you are reading this book and have not accepted Jesus as your Lord and Savior, I hope you will do so. I want you to receive the free gift of salvation that God offers to all people. Acknowledge Him and accept Him into your heart. It is my prayer that those who read this book who may be lost will have seeds planted in their hearts and that God will perform a mighty work in their lives.

My boys were very active in sports. Logan was a very good baseball player. He was a pitcher and first baseman. He was incredibly talented as a pitcher, but his promising career at this position was cut short because of a UCL tear in his elbow. He would have arm surgery following his sophomore year of high school. This type of surgery has a long period of recovery, so he could not pitch his junior year. We hoped he would return to his talent level going into his senior year, but he was never the same. He also showcased exceptional skills as a defensive first baseman and hitter, earning a scholarship opportunity to play in college. He would play for one year and then transfer to another school to complete his degree, as he had only one or two courses left for his intended degree due to all the prior college coursework he completed in high school.

Larson was also very talented in baseball, but he sustained injuries in each of his sophomore, junior, and senior seasons of high school. He had to have a major knee surgery before his junior year due to a freak sliding accident (into a base) just prior to the season in the fall of the school year. Going into that season, he had interest from a Division I school. A coach from that school had seen him play in an Atlanta showcase tournament game. All of his injuries kept him off the field for a large portion of each of those years. He was a very good hitter and fielder. After graduating high school, he no longer had any interest in playing college baseball. The good news here is that neither of them misses the game, so that is a blessing in itself.

Logan and Larson were very busy in other sports early on but wanted to specialize as they got older. Logan also played football his 7th grade year and basketball both his 7th and 8th grade years. He picked basketball back up again his senior year. Larson played Upward basketball at our church and flag football. As you can see, we were a busy sports family, and Lindsi was involved in cheer/gymnastics, as mentioned earlier. She also played Upward basketball at our church and local-league softball. Our weeks were busy with whatever sport was in season. It definitely kept us on the run. There were some periods of exhaustion for us, trying to get everyone to practices and games, but it was a blast. We strongly supported them in whatever sports they desired to play.

I played three sports in high school: baseball, football, and basketball. Baseball was my favorite, and I played college baseball, first at a Division II school and later at a Division I school. This second school was Mississippi State University, and I played for the legendary coach, Ron Polk. I played for two years at Mississippi College on a baseball scholarship and then transferred and walked on at Mississippi State University as a pitcher.

I have only one sibling, and that is my brother. He and I are identical twins. Moreover, just like me, he played at Mississippi College and also walked on at Mississippi State. And guess what? He was a pitcher. We walked on for the 1989 season and won the outright Southeastern Conference championship that year. That same season, we lost in the finals game of the NCAA Regional, denying us a berth in the College World Series. Our school achieved a first-place ranking in the nation in the preseason poll that year and ended up in the top ten of the final poll.

I had so much fun with all of my children in the yard playing some sport. The sports varied, and it was always a great time spent together with them. Those years flew by so fast. It was a pleasure, both coaching them and also watching them later as a parent in the stands.

Now, I want to turn my attention back to Lindsi. During her battle, the boys were still playing sports. Lindsi was our priority during this time as caregivers, and we made it our mission to be there for her as much as we could, but we needed periodic breaks to get some needed rest in order to come back renewed and ready to meet her many needs. We also wanted to support the boys because they had emotional needs, and they also needed our love and care. So, we attempted to make time for them whenever possible.

We rarely missed games that our children were involved in. Of course, there were extenuating circumstances where it was not possible to attend every one of them. We would miss Logan's college baseball games later as we had to be at work, and some of his games were during the week and were scheduled earlier in the afternoons, so we missed some of those, but he understood the situation. We were still able to attend a lot of his games. Earlier in Logan's playing years, during the sickness, Wanda and I could not both attend games. We would consult with Lindsi as to who she wanted to stay. So, we would decide that the person whom Lindsi didn't choose to stay with her would be the one to go to the game.

I thank God that our kids were playing sports because, for me, it kept us busy in another area of life. After Lindsi got sick, going to practice, coaching a team during a game, or just getting outside to spend time with my boys was a good thing. I needed some distance from the sadness and broken heartedness of my daughter's condition. The short periods away from the darkness that her cancer bore were therapeutic. At times, feelings of depression would creep in, so to have some time away and briefly focus on the boys was healthy for me. I never forgot about my sweet Lindsi, but it gave me a temporary release point from that pang of sorrow for her suffering.

God made that possible and provided me an avenue of brief escape while also affording me the blessing of time spent with my other children. God gave me strength so that depression could not gain its foothold. It worked, as it reinvigorated me with a renewal and a readiness to go back to see my girl and be strong for her. God will make a way when a way seems nonexistent. God brought us through the entire period, but He also prepared us *before* that trial came. He continues to hold us in His loving arms, comforting us and filling our hearts with peace.

He now has Lindsi and Wanda in His arms for eternity.

Chapter 12

"HOSPITAL/CLINIC STORIES"

Lindsi spent many hours at both the hospital and clinic. One of her hospitalizations occurred when Christmas Eve was approaching. As the days drew near, Lindsi had not been cleared for discharge, and it was looking less and less promising that it would happen by Christmas Eve. Finally, we were within a day or two of it, and Lindsi was still hospitalized, with no word about a discharge. The hospital nurses attending to Lindsi were great. They were always upbeat and encouraging to Lindsi and to us. We grew anxious about spending Christmas in the hospital. Unaware, we were about to be in for a big surprise soon.

One night, just before the eve of Christmas, some nurses brought in a huge, handmade paper craft replica of a fireplace, complete with mantle, stockings, and a wood-burning fire. Each stocking had the names of each of our family members. What a wonderful surprise. These ladies made the room feel somewhat like home. Their thoughtfulness touched us, and their creativity was impressive. This project must have taken hours to complete. Later, we received a request from the hospital to write a recommendation letter for an award that was to be given out at a later date. They asked that the letter be written for Lindsi's nursing unit. Of course, it was my pleasure to submit a letter for them. I do not know if they won that award, but they were certainly deserving to be chosen for it.

Lindsi's visits to the cancer clinic were many. The nurses at the clinic were also great. They always remarked about Lindsi's pretty smile and how much it uplifted their days at work. They probably witnessed pain and sadness every work day. Lindsi's presence would always pick them up. It just speaks volumes about Lindsi's attitude and outlook. She lived an inspiring life and affected the lives of those she came into contact.

I want to turn the spotlight now on the clinical nurses. These women were so supportive and encouraging. I'm sure Lindsi felt more at ease with the caring and kindness they showed her and their efforts to make Lindsi as comfortable as they could as they attended to her. It takes special people to go into the medical field, especially those working in pediatric and children's clinics and hospitals. I often thought about these nurses and the things they had to deal with each day, working with precious children battling some form of cancer. I'm grateful for those who strive to help others to get well or feel better. Nurses are so important and are vital to the medical field. Lindsi had a great team of nurses, without a doubt. They made her visits a little more bearable with their sweet dispositions and bedside manners. They were a blessing to our entire family.

I have another story to share, and this one transpired at the hospital. I was out in the hallway, just outside of Lindsi's room, talking with someone. Suddenly, a man appeared at one end of the hallway and was walking in our direction. He was carrying a large teddy bear in his arms, and he continued toward us. Then he stopped to ask if he could walk in and visit with Lindsi for a moment. He was a complete stranger to me, as I didn't recognize him, but I told him it was fine to go inside.

I don't recall immediately following him into the room, but I went back inside before he left. As I entered, this man was standing at the end of Lindsi's bed, talking to her. And as he stood there, he began weeping. He then shared with those of us in the room that he didn't know Lindsi, but that God had called him to come and see her. He shared that he was more of a casual Christian than a devout one, and he also mentioned that he rode a motorcycle. His unannounced visit was special, and his testimony of feeling God's calling is another testament to God's power. He did not dismiss God's calling but heeded it.

So many times, we deflect opportunities to share the love of Christ and our testimony with those who need to hear it. God does not call every person to the missionary field or to go into evangelism, but He wants us to reach out and minister to the lost of this world. We don't have to go to another state or country to witness to the lost. Our mission field could be right around us.

This man stepped out in faith and answered the call of God to visit a sick little girl whom he had never met. God can do amazing works through those who are called according to His purpose, as the book of Romans tells us (Rom. 8:28). We need to listen to His voice, answer His call, and be used to fulfill His plan for that moment. God used this man for a purpose. I don't know for certain exactly what purpose was fulfilled for God at that time, but something was achieved for Him. Maybe this man's visit touched the heart of Lindsi and lifted her up. So, that could have been the purpose or one of God's purposes. I do know that I was thankful for him, his movement to God's call, his gift of the teddy bear, and his faithfulness. May we all seek to honor our Heavenly Father and seek to bring all glory to Him.

I have one final story to share, and this one took place back at the cancer clinic. Lindsi had a scheduled appointment that day, and shortly after we arrived and got her signed in, a woman walked out of her office, which was near the sign-in desk. She greeted us and told us she was a social worker and that she helped with the Make-a-Wish Foundation. She then asked us if Lindsi would like to receive a wish. We, of course, had heard of this program, but we had limited knowledge about how it actually worked. I knew that only children with terminal illnesses were eligible.

Upon hearing the name, instead of acknowledging the offer, it pricked my heart. I then asked the caseworker about the program only being for terminally ill patients. At this point, I did not see Lindsi as a terminally ill child. She was receiving treatments to end her cancer and to be healed. So I, point-blank, asked her if this program was only for patients who were not expected to live much longer. Honestly, I don't recall her reply to me. Her offer absolutely devastated me, as I took it as my daughter's death sentence. This deflated my hope.

At that moment, I wondered if the doctors were no longer hopeful of a cure, and, if so, what was the point of all the treatments that were destroying other things in her body? I refused to believe or accept the possibility of losing Lindsi. Wanda and I had held out hope for a long time until the doctors told us there was nothing else they could do for her and that she had only a brief time left. My heart ached at the mention of a wish, but this was not about me. I was being selfish in my thought process and should have only been thinking of Lindsi. She was still there with us, so I needed to concentrate on her alone, not on her sickness. We knew she would like to have a wish before being asked. I do wonder how this made her feel, though. I wasn't going to tell her this might have meant that she would not be cured.

We asked Lindsi about it, and she, of course, wanted a wish. The next step would be for her to decide what wish she wanted to receive. They gave Lindsi some ideas on things to consider. A trip somewhere looked to be out of the question with her current condition. After some contemplation, Lindsi decided she wanted a laptop computer. After that, this lady went right to work to set things in motion.

Later, we received word that there was a company about an hour or so away that wanted to grant Lindsi's wish. Lindsi was not feeling well around this time but she was determined to make the trip to the office of the company granting her wish. She had dealt with so many long, exhausting trips for appointments, hospital visits, and treatments. She was a trooper, though, and she was going to attend her wish party.

The day arrived, and it was a rainy one, but the trip was okay for Lindsi. When we arrived, the rain had ceased, and we were able to get Lindsi out and into the building. As we entered the office building, Lindsi was greeted with what seemed like a surprise birthday party. Decorations filled the large open area. There was a large crowd of company employees, and they treated Lindsi like a queen. They showered her with gifts. I think they had pizza and other food there for us and the employees. They also had ice cream and a big cake for Lindsi. Everyone was so nice. I don't remember how long our visit lasted, but all of us had a great time. The boys were able to go with us as well, so our whole family got to share in the celebration for Lindsi. All of it overwhelmed us.

Their kindness and desire to make this day possible as well as special for Lindsi was very humbling. And, yes, she got a laptop, a pink one. This was her favorite color. Later, we spent hours at home going through all the gifts lavished on her. The company even gave the family gifts.

Lindsi received so many gifts during her sickness. These gifts and the outpouring of love for her were a sight to behold. The time spent with those employees was an uplifting time for our family. Their generosity, along with that of so many other people, touched our hearts. It was incredible to experience all the prayers and support from those we knew and those we didn't know. We marveled at God's blessings, and we will be forever thankful for them.

Chapter 13

"MORE STORIES"

Lindsi used to act out scenes pretending to be a schoolteacher. One day, I walked into the living room, where she was playing out a scene. I just stopped whatever it was I was doing and watched her in action. She was thoroughly engaged in the performance, and though she was aware of my presence, she continued her show. Lindsi was standing in front of the fireplace hearth and walking from side to side, giving out instructions to her make-believe students. She was very animated and really poured herself into her chosen role of the teacher. She would raise her voice as she pretended to scold some students for their misbehavior. She put on quite the show and was very entertaining. I enjoyed watching her become fully engrossed in playing her part as the teacher.

There is no doubt in my mind that she would have been an outstanding educator if she had chosen that profession later in life. She had such a nurturing presence about her. This trait would have served her well as a teacher. But God had His eternal plan in place and mapped out for her. Her life would be brief, but she was a success in life because she left a great legacy behind. God blessed us with the time we shared with her. We have fond memories of her to cherish.

People spoke about Lindsi's influences on their lives and the lives of others. They recall her sweet and caring spirit and her strong desire to help others. She possessed a rare characteristic that seemed so uncommon in children. You will see this positive attribute fully displayed in the following story from a former teacher's aide.

This aide shared a story about Lindsi as an elementary school student. Each day, Lindsi would go into the teacher's lounge and fetch coffee for some of the other teachers at the school. I do not know how this became a daily function for Lindsi, but she carried out the requests, nonetheless. Not only did she get them coffee, but she would go to each teacher and ask each of them, specifically, how they wanted their coffee prepared. She wanted to make sure that each of them enjoyed their coffee. What a wonderful example of servanthood.

Lindsi truly lived out what God expects of us as believers. The two greatest commands in the Bible are to love God with all of our being and to love others as we love ourselves (Mark 12:30-31). Loving all others is a difficult command for us, but if we truly love God, then we should treat all others the way we desire to be treated. Lindsi out poured her love for God through the ways she cared for and loved others. May we pursue to do the same in our daily walk.

Lindsi eventually could no longer continue attendance at her elementary school. I had a meeting scheduled with the school principal regarding the plan for her after her inability to go to school. The school was very understanding and made accommodations for Lindsi to continue with her schoolwork from home, if possible. They allowed us to work with Lindsi in trying to keep up with the work and class curriculum. This plan worked for a time, but eventually, Lindsi was no longer physically nor mentally equipped to continue. Defeating cancer became her concern—and ours. So, after that, our efforts would be put forth toward that single goal.

Lindsi tried as hard as she could to keep up with the schoolwork. Her desire and determination spoke volumes as to her character. She worked intently to achieve any goal she set out to accomplish. Lindsi fought her cancer with that same determination, and she demonstrated so much courage and inner strength through much adversity. She faced obstacles every day, yet continued to fight to the very end. She inspired a large audience that followed her story. If even one life was changed during this tragic period of our life, it was a life that was changed by God through Lindsi. A plan was already in place, and He was always in control of the situation. He was always at the wheel and made His presence known to us. He was glorified through it all.

This next story, again, reveals the genuineness of Lindsi's giving spirit. Before her bed confinement, Lindsi spent much time on one of the living room couches or our bed when she was able to avoid hospitalizations. She liked to keep herself busy doing things during those times. She and I liked to play a certain phone app word game together. Anything I could do with Lindsi or for her that would bring her a modicum of comfort or happiness was my goal. But, the most important thing to me was spending as much time as I could with her.

We enjoyed those times whenever she felt like doing things. I welcomed it and held dear every minute with her. There were times when she felt so bad and yet, she would still, somehow, show me a smile. It would just warm my heart and temporarily ease some of my sorrow and feelings of absolute helplessness gripping me in those moments.

Another one of her favorite things to do would be to get the phone out and call people. She loved to call other family members daily when she was at home. It was a wonderful blessing to watch and listen to her carry on conversations with them. Lindsi would always inquire about their day and how they were feeling. She was a sick child but was contacting others to check on them and their well-being. This was yet another example of Lindsi putting others ahead of herself, even though she was battling for her life against cancer. Wow, a little girl with a life-threatening illness, showing concern for others.

When I tell people about Lindsi, I often remark that she was an angel on earth. Her relationship with God was evident, and she connected with other people in her abbreviated life through the outpouring of her love and concern for them. Another part of Lindsi's epitaph reads: "An Angel on Earth, Now in Heaven."

Back some years ago now, our church hosted a Father/Daughter Banquet, which was held in our church fellowship hall. We got all dressed up for the event. We were all smiles as we looked forward to this time of just her and me together. It was essentially a date night out with my beautiful daughter. The fellowship hall had been fancily decorated. Upon the arrival of all guests, a picture was snapped of all the daughters with their dads. We had a great time that night.

Looking back on it, I wish I had made more of those date nights with her before her illness and wonder if she and I would have planned future date nights if she had not been diagnosed with cancer. Thoughts like these enter my mind from time to time, but I don't allow myself to dwell on them.

As stated before, I, at times, still selfishly want both her and Wanda back here with me and the family, but our future heavenly reunion quickly erases my desire for them to come back to us here. Nothing in this world compares with what awaits us in Heaven.

My thoughts refocus on the eternal. Lindsi, and now Wanda, are celebrating an eternal banquet, and it is not a one-or-two-hour gala like the one that Lindsi and I attended that night. Theirs is a celebration and worship of the one who created us, and one day, those saved by God's grace through the death and resurrection of His son, Jesus, will be a part of it. I can only imagine the splendor and joy shared by my two loves there. I'm thankful for that precious moment in time shared with Lindsi that night at the banquet, and one day, we will attend many banquets together as a family of God.

Lindsi loved to sing, and she was a member of the children's choir at the church we attended. Although she had a beautiful singing voice, she shied away from singing solos, but she certainly didn't mind singing by herself at home. I still remember her sweet voice. Her singing voice inflected such a heartfelt and genuine purpose. She was really "in the moment" when she sang. It was a joy to watch and listen to her.

When Lindsi was sick, there was a particular song she liked to sing. The name of the song was "Sanctuary." She loved this song. The lyrics of the song really captured the essence of how Lindsi lived her life. One day, I asked her to sing this song so I could record it on my cell phone. I recorded her at least twice, and each time she sang it, you could sense the sincerity and thoughtfulness in her voice. It was both moving and touching to me. I also wanted to keep her recordings as a memento. I wanted to have a vocal timepiece that I could revisit. This would be one way that I could keep Lindsi close to my heart if it were God's plan to call her home.

I eventually lost those recordings after a mishap with my cellphone. I mistakenly left the phone somewhere on my vehicle one night. I remember I was getting ready for a baseball game and just forgot to pick it back up as I left to go to the ball field. It would later fall off my vehicle as I traveled back home and as discovered later, landed on a major highway. Wanda used her phone to locate it. She brought it home, and it had been run over. The phone was beyond repair, so I had to purchase a new one and could not recover the recordings.

Before that phone was destroyed, I listened to those recordings often after her passing and each time I replayed them, I was brought to tears, but I felt this was one way that I could feel her presence in her earthly absence.

I still hold Lindsi in my heart. Losing her voice recordings saddened me, but I still have sweet memories and many mementos to hold on to. It helps me to reconnect with her. Even now, I can still recall her beautiful voice. I'm sure Lindsi is singing heavenly praises to God and that her voice is even more beautiful than before.

I encourage parents who read this book to acknowledge their children and cherish them. Don't take them for granted. Seek to appreciate the gifts and talents that God has given them and encourage them to use those talents to serve God and bring glory to Him. Lindsi used her talents in this way. She made me a very proud but humbled father. I thank God for choosing me to be her father.

The last story of this chapter is still one that brings tears to my eyes, especially when I relay it to other people. It was the most remarkable act of Godly devotion that I have ever witnessed as a father. This recounting is a testament to Lindsi's love for God.

At one point, our church had a youth program that met on Sunday nights. It was called AWANA. It is an acronym that stands for "Approved Workmen Are Not Ashamed." This program included a time of fun and games and usually concluded with a period of Bible scripture recitation. Each participant was given a book that contained Bible verses. There were many passages from God's word that the youth had to recite to adults who volunteered to sit, listen, and verify the children's correct recitation of those verses.

During this time, Lindsi was sick, but she was at home, so she was determined she was going to take part in this program, regardless of her circumstances. She could not attend the meetings because of her condition, but she wanted to work on her recitations. She would ask me to sit down by her and help her with memorization of verses for the week. I marveled at her determination to memorize the verses as she dealt with her brain cancer. We would work along gradually until she could recite a verse. As sick as our child was, without having hardly any energy to expend, she made the most unbelievable request.

The request, in itself, was an easy one if coming from the mouth of a healthy child—but not from Lindsi. She wanted to get ready, be picked up, and put in her wheelchair, then be removed again to be put in the van—and then be taken to the church to recite the verses she had learned. I could not believe her request, but we made it happen that night. Actually, God was the source of it taking place. We were able to get her into the van and take her to church.

Once there, we had one of the AWANA volunteers walk out to the van, and Lindsi recited her verses. Just learning those verses at home was not enough. She went the extra mile, just like she did to help others. How could she be both physically and mentally able to achieve this? It was through her love for God and His grace and power.

In her condition, it seemed impossible to accomplish what she did, but she had an amazing faith in God and a strong will and determination to serve Him. These things made her desire a reality. What an awesome example of her devotion to God.

We can learn spiritual lessons from children. Jesus spoke about us coming to Him as a child and having the faith of a child (Matt.18:3). I thank God for Lindsi's faith. I wonder if Lindsi's act of devotion inspired the other youth of our church that night, as well as adults.

May the way we live our lives serve as inspiration to others and that they see Jesus in us. I believe Lindsi accomplished this for God in her life.

Photographs

Our Wedding Day [Top Left]; My precious children—Lindsi, Larson (in the middle), and Logan [Bottom Right].

I don't know what Larson is looking for [Top Right], Christmas Time [Right Center], Our dating days [Bottom Right].

One of my favorites [Top Left], Honeymoon Pic [Top Right], My beautiful Bride [Bottom].

Lindsi smiling while Larson sleeps in the high chair [Top left], My sweet princess [Left Middle/bottom], Lindsi loved to cheer [Right].

Lindsi enjoyed softball, too [Bottom Right].

I arranged this shelf in Lindsi's bedroom [Left], My two beautiful girls [Top Right], Lindsi loving on her brothers. So sweet [Right-2], Fun at the Beach [Right-3], Family Photo [Bottom Right].

Some of my favorite pictures with Lindsi [Top Left], Baseball runs in our family [Top Right], Some of Lindsi's trophies [Middle Right].

Another honeymoon pic of Wanda [Top Left], The jacket Wanda has on is the one I wore as a baseball player for the Mississippi State Bulldogs [Bottom Right].

One of our engagement pics [Top Left].

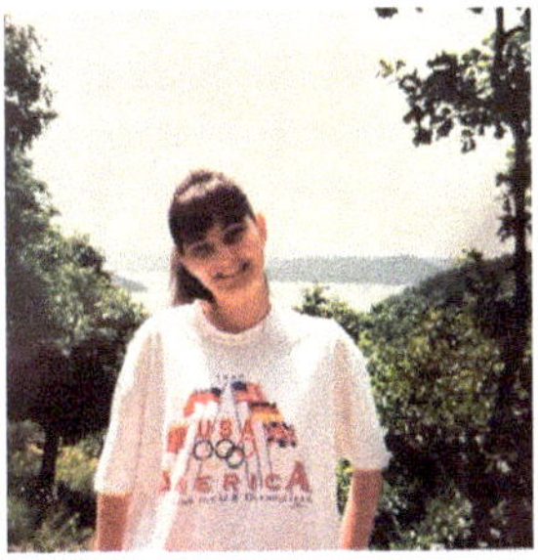
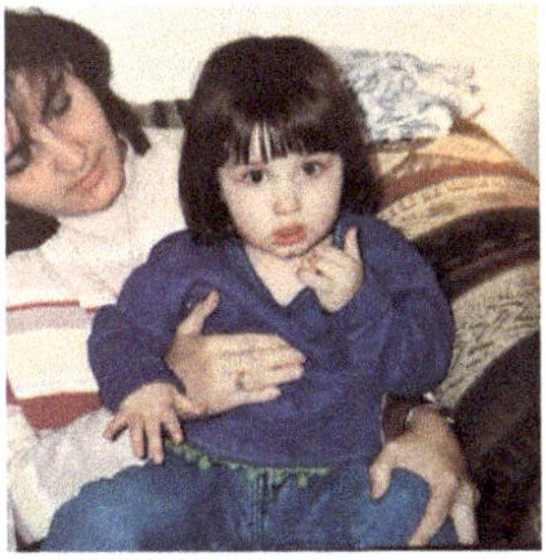
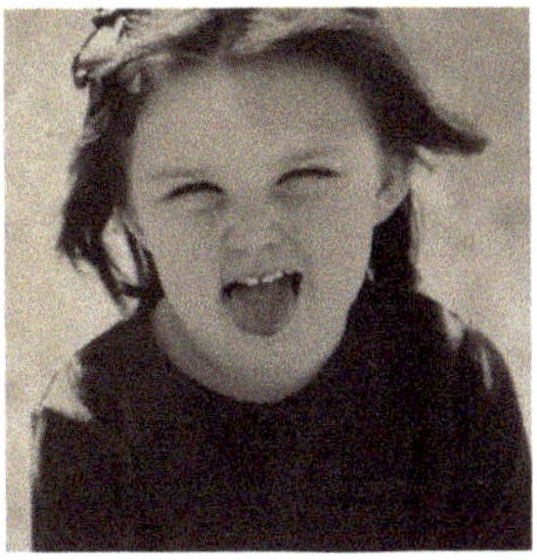
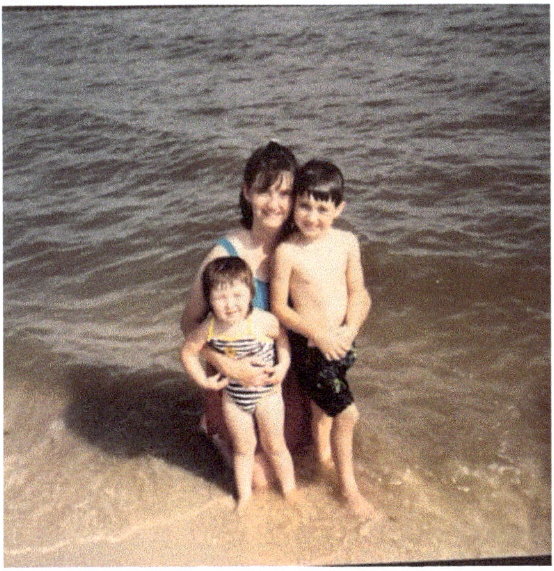
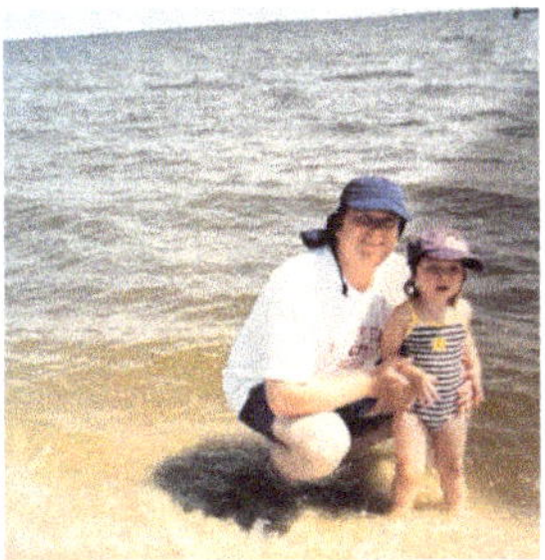
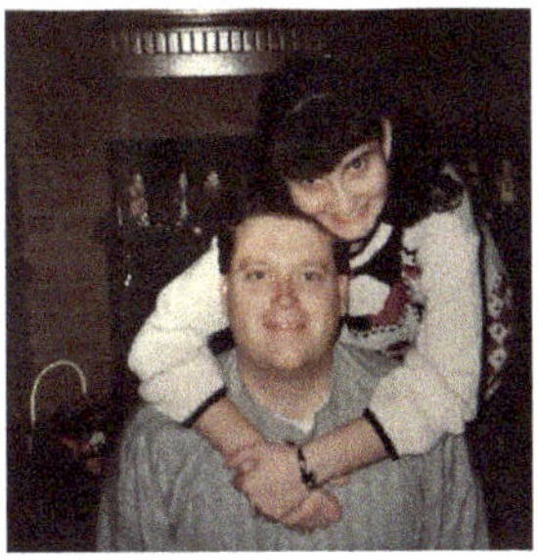

Sweet pic of my three [Top Left], Beautiful [Bottom Left], Taken after our wedding [Top Right].

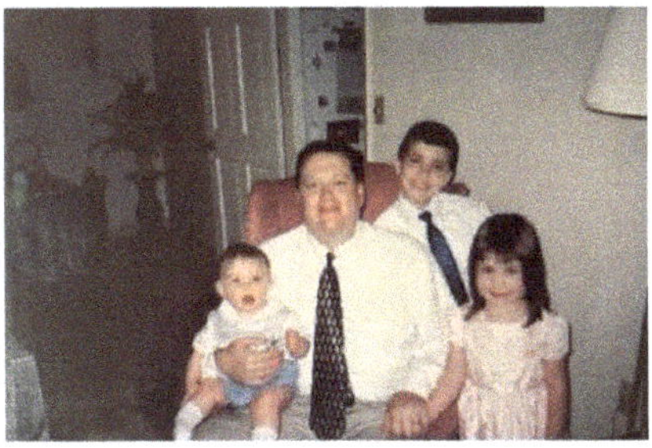
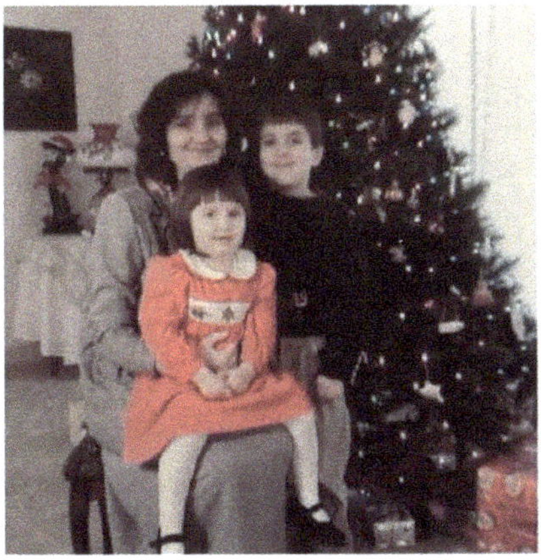
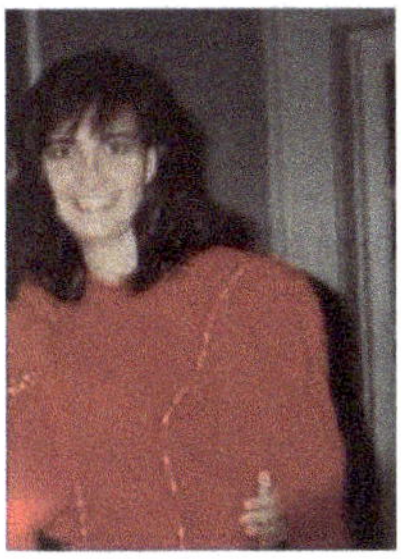
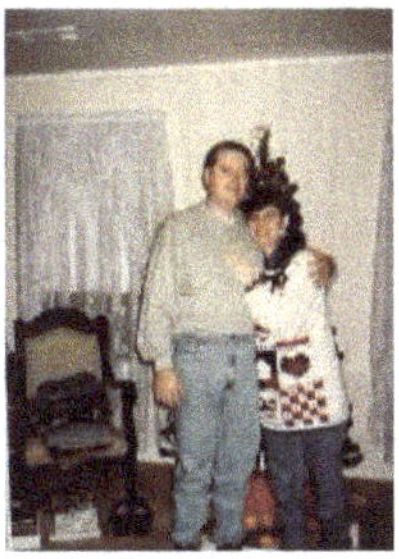
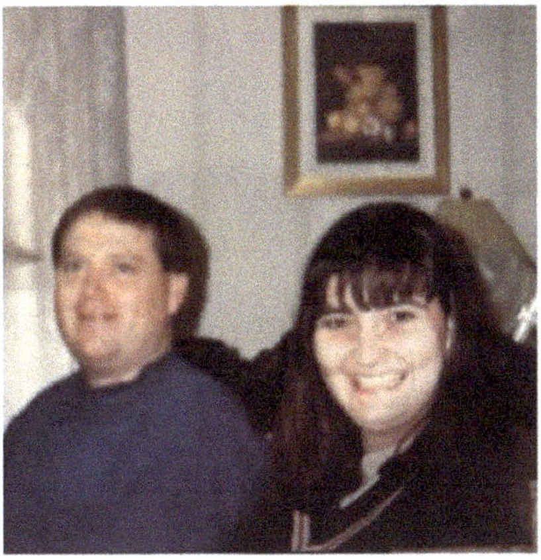
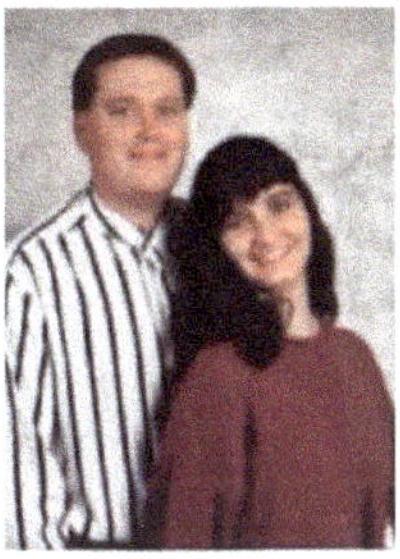
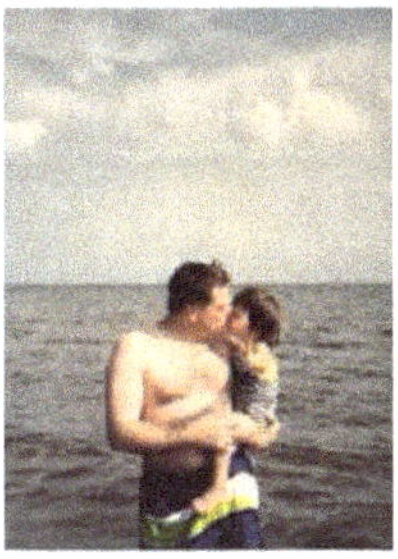

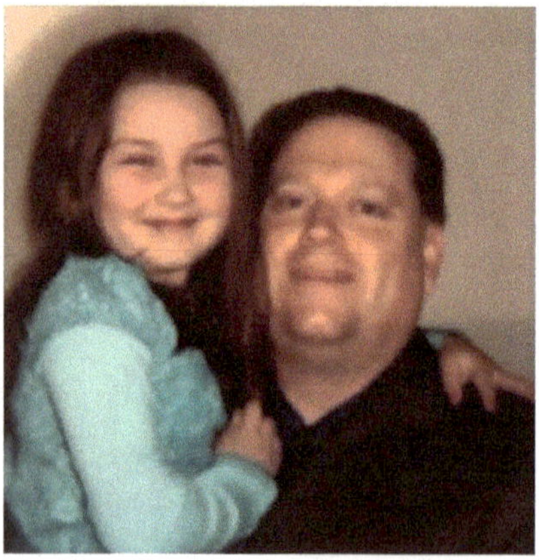

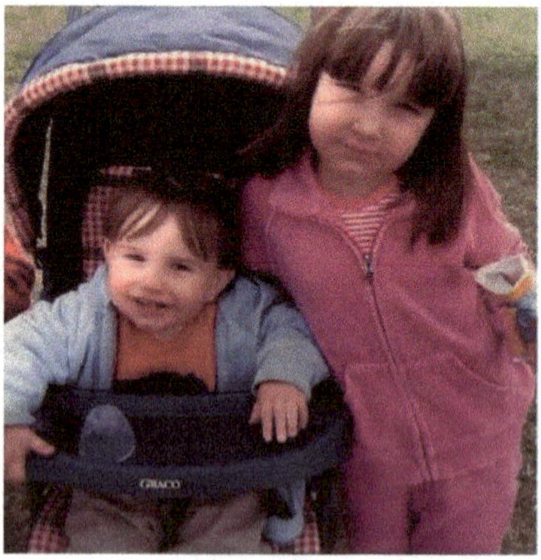
GRACO

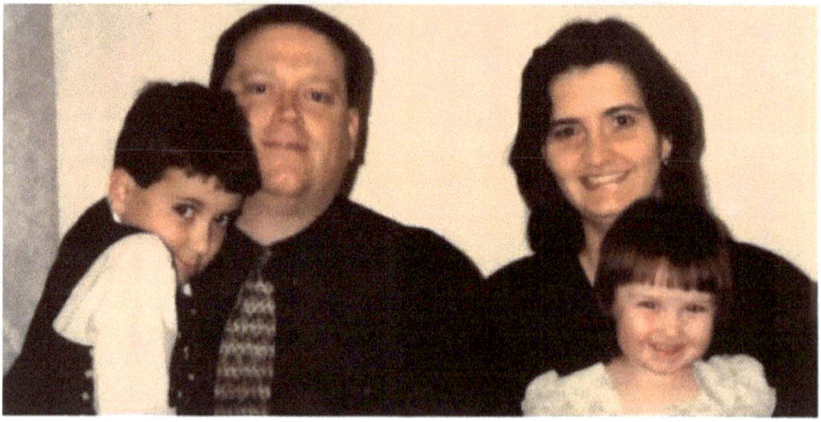

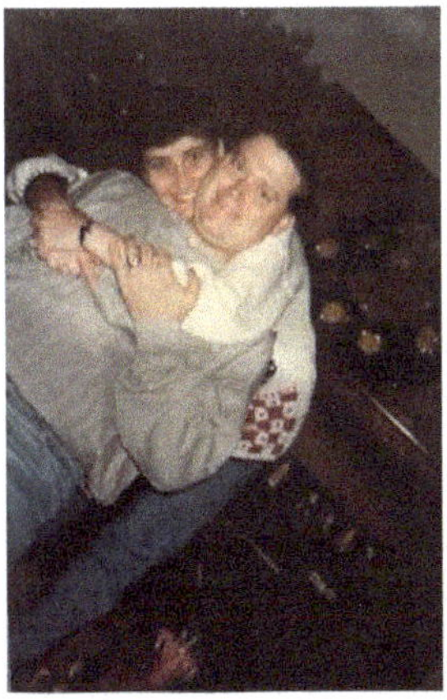
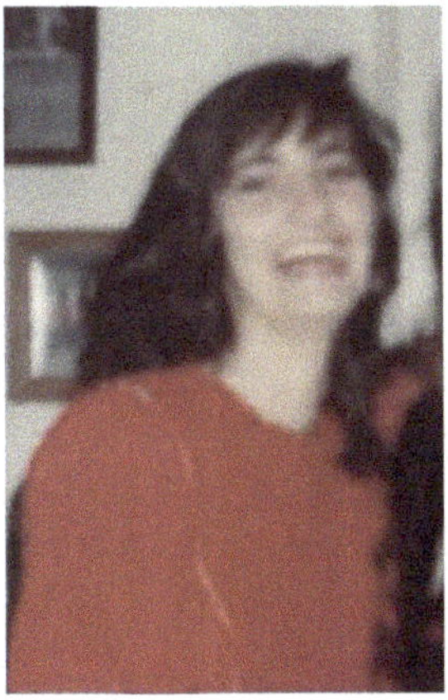
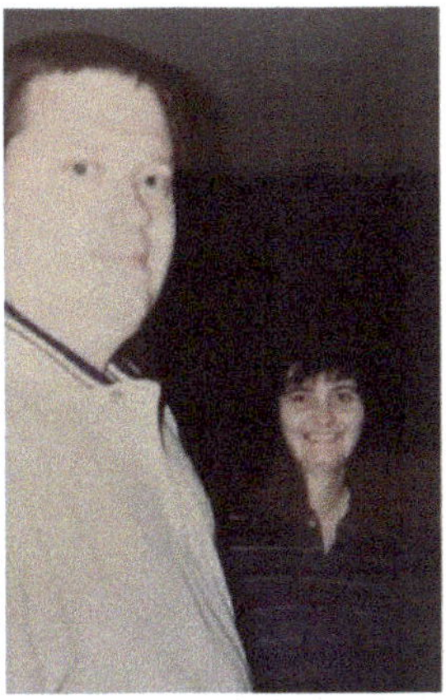
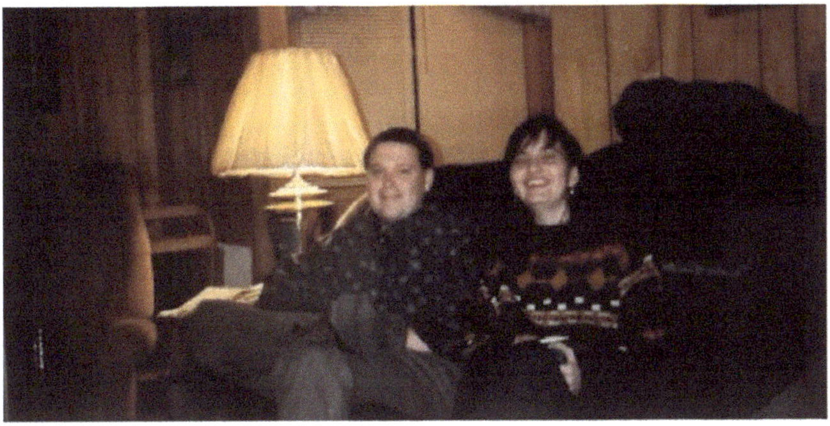

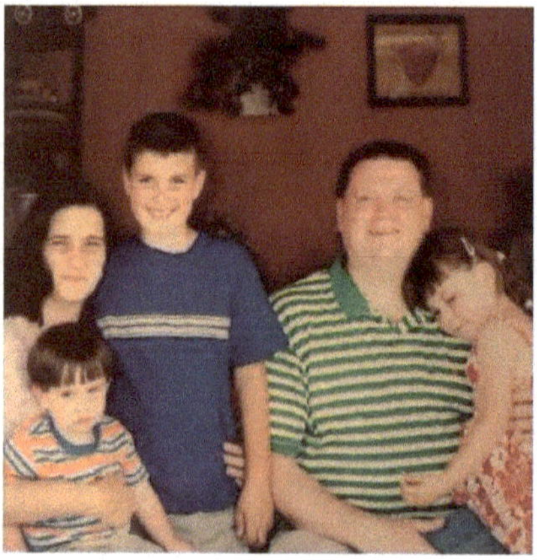

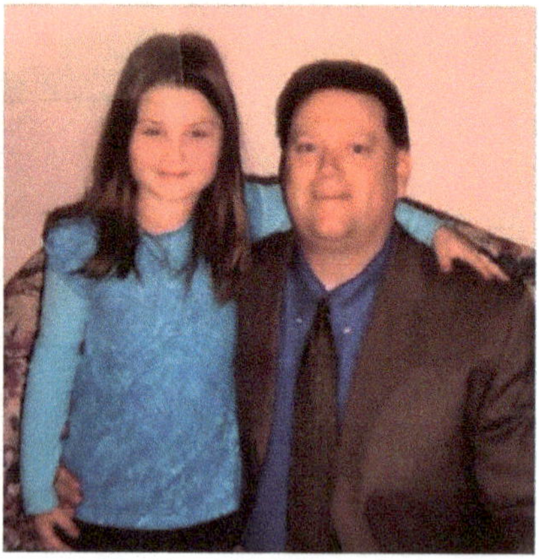

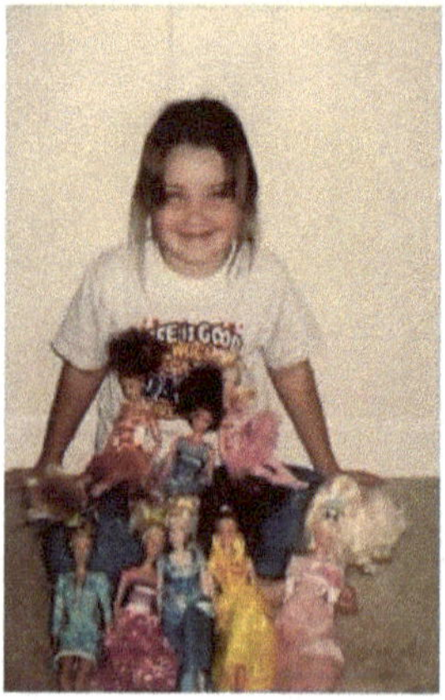

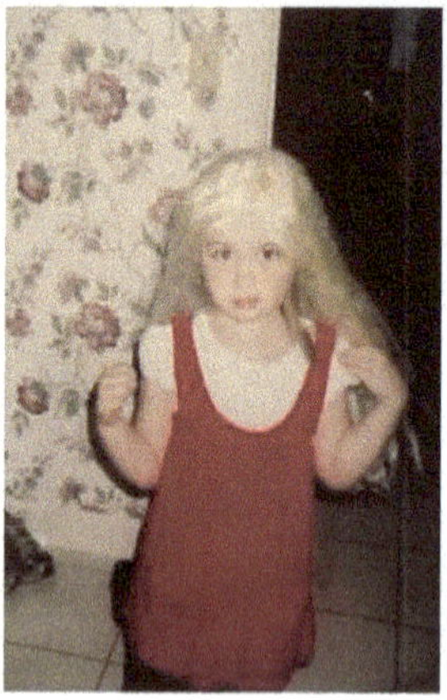

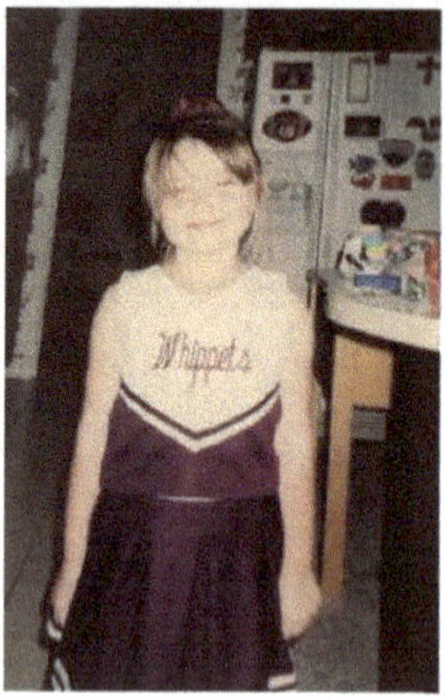
Whippets

My boys and me. Logan to the left, and Larson on the right. This pic is from 2023.

Father's Day Weekend 2024.

Chapter 14

"JOURNALING"

We were receiving so many phone calls and calls from other family members daily, wanting updated reports on Lindsi. I had heard about a website called CaringBridge, which allowed users to go online and post updates. These updates would then become available for other people to view by visiting the site. I decided I would set up an account and start posting immediately. This would be my introduction to journaling.

Word, apparently, got around quickly that I had started a CaringBridge website for Lindsi. This website would serve as a daily journal for me, and it would also be a great resource for people to stay informed. Once I began posting, I did so about every day. I was happy to learn of the site, and it aided us tremendously with less frequent calls about Lindsi's condition.

Writing became somewhat therapeutic for me. It would also serve as a daily timeline of Lindsi's journey. Many people were now being updated. People began leaving encouraging comments for Lindsi and the family. This became a useful tool and also a way to express myself to so many concerned about Lindsi.

I wrote constantly, at one point, on the site. I would later get my CaringBridge journal printed in book form through this same website. Utilizing it also minimized the dialogue needed to constantly repeat a report on Lindsi. Sometimes, we were inundated with so much information at one time, and it was hard to remember every single detail.

At times, I would write several posts a day. It was always exciting to have good reports to share. It was a joy to read the encouraging responses. They were very uplifting, and we appreciated all the replies and the time taken by people out of their busy schedules to seek out reports.

I was excited to get all of my CaringBridge journal entries and many replies compiled in a bound book. Upon receiving the book, it reminded me, again, of the sadness we experienced, but it also brought back the remembrances of the blessings God bestowed on us and how He brought the family through all of that pain and sorrow. God provided us with His strength to endure it.

The prior time that I had looked at this journal was before I had it bound. I stored it away after opening the box to make sure that it was the correct order. It had been wrapped in clear plastic, so I put it back in the box, unopened. As I was getting closer to compiling all of my writings, I unwrapped the book. My thought was to extract some of my entries and add them to the manuscript.

I had forgotten how this book looked. The front and back cover was well- designed. There were pictures of Lindsi on the cover. Then I opened the book, and the interior pages had pictures of her. The layout of the entire book looked great. Then, I began picking out some entries at random, as well as notes from those who visited the website.

I must confess that after reading just a few of them, I had to stop because I didn't want to stir up those painful memories again that I had tried to suppress. I then immediately closed the book and put it away. The pain is still there, but God empowers me to push through it, and He imbues me with His comfort and peace to overcome it.

I often try to disengage my thoughts of her sickness and replace them with those of the health Lindsi once enjoyed. She lived an exemplary life, and now, she is well for eternity. Her pain and suffering are no more. Those are the thoughts that I try to retain. I also try to keep them captivated toward the eternal. In faith, I believe Lindsi was made whole again once she left this Earth.

Praise God for our salvation through faith in Him.

Chapter 15

"MEMENTOS"

One type of gift that Lindsi received in great quantity was blankets. Lindsi put these items to great use. I still have them stored away, with some still in use.

One blanket, in particular, brings back memories of Lindsi each time I see it or use it. It is special to me because it was her favorite. Its patterns consist of large multi-colored circles with a white background. The colors are vivid and really stand out on the blanket.

We have pictures of Lindsi wrapped up in blankets, smiling from ear to ear. She loved her blankets. It's wonderful to have mementos like these. Mementos can reconnect us to our loved ones. When I see her blankets, I choose to remember the smiles and small comforts these blankets brought her instead of the need for them during her sickness.

God knew just what Lindsi needed during her struggle with brain cancer, and He used those who gave Lindsi the gifts of blankets. He made His presence felt, and He blessed Lindsi with these gifts she truly needed through the generosity of so many. His mighty hand was at work, and it was showcased in our journey that He planned for Lindsi and for us. We are called to be the hands and feet for our Savior. We should seek daily to live for Him and meet the needs of those around us.

Many people heard about Lindsi's cancer crisis. They took notice and sprang into action by fulfilling the needs of our entire family. They helped us in so many ways. Some graciously donated money, some cooked meals for us, some showered Lindsi with gifts, and many prayed for her and for us. They heeded the call to aid us in our long journey. We were so humbled by this outpouring of love shown toward us. Not only did God use humanity to show us His goodness, but He also used fellow believers to bring honor and glory to Himself. His love was magnified through the graciousness of many individuals. The part they played in God's plan was a demonstration of their love for God.

God left our family with wonderful mementos, and He has allowed us to hold on to the memories of our lost ones. He left a place in our hearts for both Lindsi and Wanda to remain in spirit. God has filled the void I sometimes feel deep inside me and continues to fill it with His overflowing peace. He comforts my soul with the gift of the Holy Spirit.

God has been so good to me and my sons as we continue to deal with our losses. Our hearts still ache for their physical absence from us, but God is always there to pick us up when we are feeling low. He is there, and the blanket mementos are proof that He has our best interest at heart. He knew the blankets would be one of the things Lindsi would need. This blessing was just one of the many signposts of His provisions and love for us.

If you are struggling with the loss of a loved one or loved ones, I pray you lean on God for healing and, if you don't know Him, that you will surrender to Him and accept Him. Then you can experience the peace that is beyond all human understanding.

The number of gifts that Lindsi received was overwhelming, but so appreciated. A time later, Wanda and I would sort back through all the extensive gifts, then box some of them and store them away. I still live in the home that we last purchased. There is a long, expansive great room in the front of the house, just by the foyer into the home. Part of this room became a storage area for a large portion of Lindsi's gifts. We had to move some of it to this area in order to have more living space.

Even though our house was large, it quickly filled up. The house has great storage spaces all throughout, but it was already about filled to capacity before all the gifts started coming in. The generosity extended to Lindsi and the family from so many people was incredible.

I wondered, sometimes, how Wanda and I were going to go about sorting through it all. Tending to Lindsi took up most of our days, so time spent doing other things like this was limited, but decisions had to be made as to the reallocation of storage for some gifts in order to create more living space in those areas we used the most.

The great room turned out to be that area of storage. After Lindsi passed away, about half of that room was stacked. In fact, you could not walk over to one wall as there were no open rows to be found to walk through. Boxes blanketed one side of that room. Any visitors who may have made their way back to this room may have mistaken us for hoarders. I must admit, part of this room looked like that of hoarders. We rarely discarded anything. Much of the storage items were true mementos that signified the wonderful generosity and goodness of others. Letting go of objects such as these can be quite difficult.

Some memento pieces might not seem like much to a casual observer, but they can hold great significance to the one to whom it was given. These items still hold a place in our hearts because it was a reminder of a specific moment or special time in our lives. It holds an emotional attachment to us. But sometimes, we need to let go of some things and realize that a physical object cannot truly fill the emptiness inside, and we need to turn to a spiritual source for our peace. Our dependence for help should be on God and Him alone.

I have certainly leaned on God through the losses I suffered in my life, and I want to cling to the happy memories of Lindsi and our family. I try to maintain memories of the good times our family shared. Lindsi was a wonderful daughter, and Wanda was a great mother. I try not to let the negative thoughts outweigh the positive ones.

Remembrances are what we have left of loved ones who have left this Earth. Material things only promote the memories of others, not their losses. Lindsi's smile and sweet, loving spirit cannot be replaced. I have parted with some of Lindsi's mementos, such as teddy bears, which I offered to other family members, especially nieces and nephews. They took some of them, but there are many more that I still have displayed in the house.

God enters our hearts through His Holy Spirit and fills us with His love and care. Nothing else will satisfy us or ease our pain. If we call upon Him, He will meet us and sustain us. To know that He is always there is so comforting. Whether our needs are great or small, He is there to help us. He is there to care, share, and bear our sorrows in life. He wants to dwell in us always, but we have to open up our hearts to receive it and to enjoy the blessings He has for us. We cannot shut ourselves off from God and expect to handle the burdens of life on our own.

Losing Lindsi and Wanda was tragic, but God never moved in those moments of despair. He was present the entire time. I still need His comforting each day and night, and He never fails to provide it. The power of God was revealed in our life struggles. His divine sovereignty was magnified. I give God all the glory and honor for His goodness and grace extended to us in our time of travails and struggles.

Earlier, I mentioned Lindsi's beautiful brownish-blonde hair. She started to lose her hair after receiving her chemotherapy and radiation treatments. I know that some cancer patients consider wearing wigs or some type of other headwear, like caps or hats. Lindsi chose the latter. She was beautiful in whatever she wore to us. She received several of these, along with some knitted caps for cold weather, and she would wear them occasionally. People gave her all kinds of stuff, and all the gifts were very thoughtful, as they were those things that she could truly use.

I stated earlier the plethora of storage spaces throughout our home. God blessed us with a four-bedroom, three-bath house. We moved into this house years before Lindsi got sick. I still have some of Lindsi's clothes that are still hanging in her closet or stored away in space bags. As wonderful as all the gifts were to Lindsi, they are now mementos. Most of them leave positive memories, while others leave some painful ones. Again, I try to focus on the positive and not let myself get caught up in the negativity. It's not healthy to let the mind dwell on the pain. Instead, one needs to focus on the goodness of times shared with their loved ones. For me, this is my aim each time I deal with this struggle.

Lindsi was gifted some fancy hats, and she wore them often. Of course, her hats had another purpose other than hiding her hair loss. They also protected her from the harmful rays of the sun. She could travel some and watch Logan play baseball, so we always made sure that her head was covered when outside. I know it meant so much to Logan to have her there at his games. Logan loved his sister so much, and he was proud to be her brother.

Stuffed animals were one of the most common gifts Lindsi received. They came in all different shapes and sizes. Most of these toys are now stored in space-saver bags, and others are proudly displayed on her bed. As mentioned earlier, I gave some of these stuffed toys away, but many remain. These gifts represented people's kindness and goodness, and they also brought a little joy to Lindsi, too. Certain ones have sentimental value to me personally, so I have held on to those.

Eventually, I will need to make some decisions on what to do with these to free up some additional space in the house and to enable myself to move on from the painful memories they sometimes bring back. One of my plans is to pass them on to any future grandchildren, God willing. This way, they can enjoy them and also learn more about their late aunt and the great legacy she left for God. Also, these physical objects can tell the story of the generosity of others and their love and admiration for Lindsi.

Mementos are important to serve as a link to the past, but they don't replace the person who was lost. They only help us have remembrances. They can give us enjoyable ones to recall.

I have many pictures of Lindsi prominently displayed throughout the house. For example, I have three framed, enlarged photographs of just Lindsi and me hanging in my bedroom, just above a dresser. I put them in that precise location, as I often stop in front of it, putting up clothes, retrieving my wallet, or getting some clothing out to wear for the day. So, that way, I might pause for a moment and lift my eyes just a little up on the wall and gaze at my sweet princess.

Each picture was taken during different ages of her life. I have a baby picture up to an older-age photo arranged from left to right. One is a picture of me holding her when she was a baby. She was so precious, with a cute little bonnet on her head. The next picture was taken just after a school program she took part in, and I was kneeled down beside her. That day, her pretty hair was in pigtails. The last photo is one of my absolute favorites. She and I were sitting on a sofa, hugged up together.

Pictures aid me in keeping her memory alive and continuing to hold her in my heart. At times, I will take long looks at some of these pictures and receive a sense of comfort as I look upon her smile. Now, I do the same with pictures of my beautiful wife, Wanda. I transformed a small end table and adorned it with pictures of us and the family, and I also have a framed poem I wrote for Wanda years earlier. I wrote several poems to her over the years.

And then, there are those pictures of Lindsi when she was fighting cancer. These are pictures that aren't displayed, and I never plan to have them visible. I will keep them where they are now—in a photo album. The ones taken after her treatments are so pitiful. I just can't look at these as long. This causes me to shift back to pain and heartache. I try to counter that by keeping those pictures from my sight, but instead, I temper my emotions with thoughts on her prior, healthy life.

I hold my faith in God with the belief that she is now with Him, removed from all the pain and suffering that she went through. Again, in my humanness, I sometimes become selfish and want her back with me, but it is pointless to hope for this because it was God's plan for her to be with Him after nine years of life.

Early on, I had to get to a place of acceptance, and later, I did, but I did often question God. I could not change His plan. His plan for Lindsi was deemed before her birth. Until I came to that realization, I was questioning God's omniscience. We fight a losing battle when we try to oppose God's all-knowingness. We can't see nor comprehend God's purpose in allowing awful things to happen, especially when it is upon us. In the end, God's plans are that of perfection, and those plans will never fail.

We can't think beyond, in terms of the eternal as finite beings, but we have to put our faith and trust in Him. He created us. He also sent His son to redeem us, and He also gave us victory over both sin and death.

Our lives are like mists that quickly evaporate, but our salvation after death will give us life again—but life eternally. When I look at pictures of both Lindsi and Wanda, I also reflect on the new lives they now enjoy in Heaven. I trust their departures were in God's timeline. God had a purpose in those plans, and it was perfected in each of their lives.

Most families like to take lots of photos, and we were one of them. Some photos don't always turn out so well. Lindsi was a very photogenic child, but she had her moments when the camera shouldn't have flashed. She was an emotional child at times. Some pictures of her capture that emotion, but mostly, she would express her big smile for the camera. You could see the love she had in her heart and her zest for life. In the few photos where Lindsi was crying, I think it involved her brothers on some of those occasions, but these occurred during their early childhood.

In some photographs, you can see the love she had for her family. She might have her arm around one of her brothers or her hands on their shoulders. When Larson was a baby, she liked to hold him. She was such a loving individual. Her heart was as big as her smile. I really believe that her joy was genuine, not only through her smiles but the way she conducted herself in this life. Her smile came naturally to her. She had an inward passion for helping others. She exemplified the salt and light that God wants each of us to be for Him in this world we inhabit. If we can be that for Him, we bring honor and glory to His name. God delights in our obedience and faithfulness.

We often fail in these areas, but God also offers us His grace and forgiveness when we fall. His love for us is immeasurable, and He wants us to draw closer to Him, talk to Him, and serve

Him. It was so amazing how a small girl could leave such an indelible imprint on the lives of adult individuals. Only by the power of our Heavenly Father could this be made possible.

Lindsi made herself available to be used for God's kingdom. If we are willing, then God can work through us to accomplish mighty works.

My parents still have pictures of Lindsi displayed in the living and dining room area of their home. They cherish these photos, as I do. It helps them to keep Lindsi's memory alive and to honor her. They sorely miss her. She was one of the joys of their wonderful grandchildren. Lindsi always enjoyed going to visit them to spend the night. There was plenty of space to play outside, and the kids did all kinds of things with my mom and dad.

Often, when visiting my parents, I will take some time to look at some pictures they have of Lindsi. They have some different photos of Lindsi that I don't have displayed in my home. I'm thankful for the photographs and that we have many to look back on and talk about.

I have a framed personal drawing of Lindsi from one of her school photos that someone was so kind to give us. It is beautiful, and I have it hanging in my living room. I notice it often as I walk by. These keepsakes allow us to go back in time and recall periods of happiness with our lost loved ones. I can just take a moment and gaze into Lindsi's beautiful face and see her wonderful smile. It eases some of the sadness and grants me the peace I need. The same can be said when I look at Wanda in pictures.

For some time, I would not go into the bedroom where Lindsi passed away. The memory was still so vivid, and it brought me great sadness just walking by it. Then, after some passage of time, I made my way into that room, and it became easier for me. Now, I use part of that room as an office area. In fact, I spent many hours in Lindsi's room working on the manuscript for my book. I realized I needed to confront my grief and begin moving forward again. By God's grace, I have been able to accomplish this.

Recalling Lindsi's smile brings another thought to mind. A smile can be a powerful thing. Just think about it. A simple relay of a smile to another might uplift a tough day they might be experiencing. A smile might be just the cure for making someone's day a little better. Simple acts of kindness, like a smile toward others, please God. Smiles can temporarily take away a measure of sadness another may be dealing with. Smiles may also have the potential to have as much of an impact as a spoken word of encouragement. God's word reveals to us that a merry heart is a good medicine (Prov.17:22). So, if you have a merry heart, it would stand to reason that an outward appearance would be a smile. If we are happy inside, a smile should abide.

This was true of Lindsi. She was happy inside because she believed in Jesus and accepted Him in her heart, and her smile confirmed it. She extended her love for Jesus by showing her love for others. What a testimony to the greatness of God. He can work through the lives of old and young alike in spectacular ways. He can also work through us to bring the lost into His fold. We serve a majestic God who loves us unconditionally, and He made it possible for us to reside with Him forever through the gift of His son, Jesus. Oh, the innumerable smiles there must be up in Heaven.

Through the years, I have ordered photo reprints of Lindsi and the family. I've had photos encased in customized frames and ornaments because I like to surround myself with pictures. Also, I have many photo albums Wanda and I collected over all our years together. Some displayed photos are of Lindsi and me together. Others are of just Wanda and me. At times, I'll stop by a picture and whisper an "I miss you" or "Hey, sweetie." I filled my work office with family photos, which left me with so many to take down and pack up after my retirement. I have stored away so many framed pictures of us. Hanging every one of them would leave little space on the walls inside my house.

These pictures harken back to those times of happiness, but they can also bring attention to our times of contentment changing in a flash. We felt this firsthand. Our lives were suddenly thrust into panic and, in the end, sorrow and grief. Cancer rocked our family dynamic, and it would never be the same again during her sickness or after her death. Our family priorities would change drastically, as we had to shift almost all our priorities to Lindsi for her care. Our boys were so understanding regarding this.

I want to point out here that we didn't abandon our sons during this time. We still did our best to meet their needs and showed them our love and support. It was a trying time for each family member, but God watched over us and made Himself known to us through His blessings and grace.

I briefly mentioned the photos of Lindsi taken after she had received treatments. They are difficult to look at, but, you know, I can't think of a single one where Lindsi was not smiling. Some of them were not as big as some of her others, but she managed a smile. If I look at them again, I try to focus on only her face and her smile rather than the rest of her ravaged body. She was a warrior in her fight, and she handled everything that was dealt her.

I just can't imagine how a little girl or boy would feel after being told that they had cancer and then going through any surgeries and treatments that might be required. I believe God was holding Lindsi's hand, comforting her, and preparing her for what was ahead.

Sharing this is very emotional for me. I was with her through her fight until the end, and she was the bravest and most courageous person I have ever known. She was and *is* my hero.

Cancer took her earthly life, but she defeated death and now enjoys her home in Heaven for eternity.

Chapter 16

"THE POWER OF PRAYER"

During Lindsi's illness, we were told that plans were being made to have a prayer vigil for her. The vigil would take place at our county courthouse on one of the front lawn areas. The courthouse stands at the center of our town square. As the plans were being finalized, we were not sure if Lindsi would feel well enough to attend, but by the grace and goodness of God, she was able to do so.

The courthouse was a very short distance from home, only about two miles. The day arrived, and we got ready to go for the nighttime prayer vigil service. It was chilly that night, so we got Lindsi dressed and wrapped her up in one of her favorite blankets. Upon arrival, we took her into the courthouse lobby. The courthouse has four doors fronting each side of the town square. Wanda was an elected official and served as the county circuit clerk, and her office was housed there. Lindsi was wheeled up to the door opening facing the courtyard side of the service. A large crowd was gathered on the lawn.

Our pastor spoke for a few minutes, and I was asked to speak a few words. This was very difficult for me, as I was so emotional, but I felt led to say something after being asked. I remember looking back up at Lindsi in her wheelchair during the service. It pained me terribly to see how quickly her body was failing her from the cancer and treatments. I had a heavy heart that night, along with deep sorrow, but even so, I was still hopeful for a miracle of healing for Lindsi.

At this point in time, the outlook for Lindsi was bleak, but to see so many fellow believers united together in prayer was humbling. They were holding out hope as we were that God could still perform a miracle of healing. Their presence and unison in prayer uplifted our family. The Bible affirms that the fervent prayer of just a single person avails much (Jas. 5:16). At that moment, we were in the presence of a throng of prayer warriors. This vigil meant so much to us. I'm thankful to those who attended that night and for their support and prayers. I'm also thankful for those who began praying for us during our journey.

The public support, concern, and prayers were plentiful. As already stated, people provided monetary and emotional support, brought in food and gifts, and others made things personally for Lindsi. She also received many cards and letters. God was blessing our lives through their giving spirits.

Yet, another contingency of support came in the form of signs. Someone or several people came up with the idea of having some large signs, as well as smaller ones produced. These signs simply read, "Prayers for Lindsi."

Soon, I saw these signs placed in yards. The elementary school that Lindsi last attended had a huge sign planted in front of it. Her sign would remain in some locations for a long time. I had about an hour's commute to my work position at Mississippi State University. During my travels, I would see her signs posted along the highway. It was a somber sight for me, but it also reminded me that goodness and kindness still existed in the world. How refreshing it was to witness such concern by others for Lindsi. God's light in this world was illuminated by the love and attention shown toward our daughter. His light transcended our small part of the world.

And from here, His light penetrated and expanded throughout our country and, eventually, across the world. Prayers were being lifted up for Lindsi from other parts of the world. God's work was breathtaking to behold.

Prayer is one way we communicate with God. He allows us to have fellowship with Him now without pre-appointed rituals, and we can talk with Him at any moment. Prayers were in abundance for Lindsi. I know God listened to each one, but His will would be carried out. Ask yourself this question. Am I more prayerful during times of trials and stresses in my life, as opposed to those of prosperity? Good times or bad should not dictate our prayer life or prayer patterns, but I think they do. I know I fail in my prayer life daily. We should always have a thankful heart for God's blessings. He provides blessings every moment of our lives, but we so often turn a blind eye to them.

Waking up in the morning is being granted another day of life by God. This blessing may seem insignificant to us, but a blessing is a blessing, no matter how small we see it or miss it entirely. God wants us to give our thanks to Him for the blessings He provides. Our uttered prayers should include thankfulness. Prayer should not only entail asking for God to give us things but also acknowledging Him for His power, perfection in knowing all things and being everywhere at once. He wants us to seek Him daily and talk to Him in our Christian walk. This is part of our relationship with our Heavenly Father.

Prayer is vital in our walk with God. How wonderful it is that we can pray to God through Jesus, His son, as our intercessor. Those in the Old Testament days did not have this opportunity under the Old Law. Now, under the New Law, we have a direct relationship with Him and can make our petitions known as we ask it in the name of Jesus.

Sometimes, I pray for something specific that I want, but I recognize that God will answer it in His infinite wisdom and in His timing. I know His plans will come about, not my own selfish ones. We should all come to this understanding.

I prayed for God to heal Lindsi. I believe God heard my pleas for a miracle. A miracle was not in His plans, however. Others prayed for a miracle of healing also, but the will of God will always be the result. In the end, God still healed Lindsi and made her whole again—just not in the way I or others prayed for it to happen.

My hope comes through my faith and belief that Lindsi no longer suffers, as she has received a new body in Christ and resides in eternity. God's plans serve His purposes. I'm at peace now, but I still ask for it to be granted to me each day. Through Jesus, Lindsi defeated death and now enjoys only life eternal.

We should make prayer a priority in our lives. There should be no loss for words when we enter a time of prayer, but at times, words may be lacking. I'm sometimes guilty of this in my prayer life. In prayer, we can acknowledge that God is all-powerful. We can offer thanks for His love, mercy, grace, and blessings. His blessings flow every second, minute, and hour of each day. Just thanking God for His blessings should make for an abundance of words. We should always be reverent and committed in our prayers. Some prayers may not be as verbose as others, but they should be intentional.

The Bible teaches that if we call upon God and pray, God will listen to us (Jer.29:12). I fall short of these goals of prayer often, but God wants us to take prayer seriously. Prayer can also involve being still and seeking direction and guidance from God. God can provide this for us by the Holy Spirit within us. I do ask God for His wisdom and guidance daily.

The prayers for Lindsi were many. God heard every one for her, and He blessed our family through the darkness of the trial we faced. Our Lord was sitting on His throne, and He listened intently to every word that was spoken by each person who prayed for Lindsi. God will always listen to us as we pray to Him. Every prayer lifted up for Lindsi was important to Him.

I'm thankful that God still listens to our requests. He also hears the praises of thanksgiving to Him. There were many blessings He bestowed on us each day of Lindsi's sickness. He knew her needs and ours before we ever asked. The power of prayer is real, and it can make a difference in our lives.

Chapter 17

"SAYING GOODBYE"

The days leading up to the funeral were so difficult. We had just endured the period prior to Lindsi's death, and though we knew it was going to happen, the anguish and sorrow that followed were nearly unbearable.

We had to meet with the funeral home director to make funeral arrangements and select a burial casket. Wanda and I were drained and worn out, both physically and emotionally. Having to make decisions in our grief was so hard, but it had to be done. I painfully recall the visit to the funeral home to see Lindsi for the last time before her body would be transported to our church for the funeral service. As I entered the door of the room and saw her, I burst into tears. My baby girl was now gone from this world.

Losing my sweet princess was agonizing. I couldn't wrap my arms around her anymore or hold her hand. How were we going to move on and deal with her absence? I already knew that answer deep down. I'm sure my grief clouded my outlook at that time. The answer would be my dependence on God. He was still in control as He was throughout all the awful times of Lindsi's suffering and our sadness.

We knew what was going to happen after the doctors delivered the dire news that there were no more options for Lindsi. But even though we could see the imminent outcome approaching, we were still so distraught when that time came. We didn't want her to suffer any longer, but her loss didn't lessen the grief we bore.

Still, we rested upon God's comfort and peace, and He would equip us to move forward. We also knew, in our hearts, that Lindsi wanted that of us, too. We did move on, and later, we had to do it again after losing Wanda. The boys and I also knew that our responsibility was to continue on with our lives after another loss. Wanda desired that of us, as God did.

Lindsi had the most beautiful funeral service. The flowers given in Lindsi's memory adorned the sanctuary. They were aligned on each side of her casket, in front of the pulpit. I kept some of those plants alive for a long time, but now I'm down to only one plant. I've had it for twelve years now, and it is one of my favorites.

Our pastor did a wonderful job presiding over the service. We also had other pastors, one from my home church growing up and another from a nearby church that took part in the service. The sanctuary overflowed with people.

Lindsi's visitation, the night before, took place in the church sanctuary as well, in expectation of many visitors. This location would better serve the high volume of visitors. People poured out their love and sentiments to us with words of encouragement.

We selected several songs to be played for the service. One song was "Amazing Grace." Also played was the song "Sanctuary," which was one of Lindsi's favorites. We selected "Cinderella" by Stephen Curtis Chapman as the song for a video loop running on the large video screens on each side of the pulpit. The minster of music at our church produced the video. We supplied him with some pictures that we selected from past photos. He did a great job getting it all put together. It was a wonderful memorial and tribute to our daughter. We were given a copy of the video later. I have watched it only once or twice since the funeral, and each time, my emotions were stirred again. It has been several years now since I last watched it. I try to hold on to the best memories of her now. She is still with me in spirit.

I wrote a eulogy for Lindsi that I want to share with you. Our church pastor read it during Lindsi's service. I also entitled the eulogy as well. Here is the title and eulogy in its entirety:

My Daughter, My Princess, and God's Little Angel

"My sweet princess Lindsi, God knew you before I knew you, and He had your plans laid out before He sent you to our family. You have been such a blessing and such a witness and a testimony to others who have ever met you in their lives and many others who never met you. You had such a servant heart even before you accepted Christ. You loved and cared for so many others and never put yourself ahead of others. For such a young child and not yet accepting Christ, it was so amazing to see how you lived your life. You left a wonderful legacy here on Earth. You were in God's hands then, just as you are now. You are in a wonderful place now, a place where you will live eternally with all fellow believers. I just know that you are going to be praising the Lord on high with the beautiful voice He gave you. Oh, you had the sweetest and prettiest singing voice. I enjoyed listening to you sing so much. You brought me so much joy and laughter. You had the prettiest smile in the world.

You had such an impact for God in such a short amount of time that God gave you here on Earth, and I feel that you would have been such a great witness for your Savior. I don't understand why God called you home at such an early age, but I pray that God will reveal it to me, when He so chooses.

My heart aches that you are no longer here, but I realize that you are in Heaven now with your Heavenly Father.

We are not our own. We belong to God, whether we are a child or adult. Even though I miss you dearly, I realize that you will no longer feel pain or needles or have to take any more awful medicine. You will have a new body that is holy and pure, and knowing that consoles me.

As your earthly father, I will truly miss so many things. I will not get to celebrate any more birthdays with you. I will not get to walk you down the aisle on your wedding day. I will not get to see you have children. I will not get to take you on that dinner date that I wanted to take you on after you got well. I will no longer get to see your sweet smile. I won't be able to see these things in this earthly life, but I will see you again and be with you for eternity some day in Heaven, and all the things in this world that I will miss with you will not compare to our reunion in Heaven.

I thank God for you, Lindsi. Our whole family thanks God for you. Our short time together has been wonderful, and even though this last year and several months have been full of darkness with your sickness and all of your treatments and all of your trips to the doctors' offices and the hospital, it was still just wonderful being your father. I love you with all my heart, Lindsi. I was deeply blessed to be chosen to be your father by God. You will always be my earthly daughter and my princess. Remember how often I would ask you if you were still my princess, even as you got older? There will always be a place in my heart for you, Lindsi, my princess. And now you are God's little angel with Him in Heaven, just as you were when you walked on this Earth. I know that because of the wonderful person you were and the countless people who have referred to you as an angel of God.

I love you, and your mom and brothers love you always and forever. All of us will see you again someday. Your mom and

I were so honored to be your earthly parents, and we thank God so much for that. You will never be forgotten, and know that you are loved and were loved by so many people here on Earth. You touched so many lives and made an impact for Christ. You made an impact on your family, Lindsi, in so many ways. You opened my eyes up to the things that are important, and that is to live my life always for Christ and to always put Him first.

You also taught me the importance of seeking to follow the Golden Rule and to see and meet the needs of others around me.

My life and our family's lives will never be the same. Thank you, Lindsi, for being the wonderful daughter that you were to us. We were so privileged to have had the honor of raising you. The hurt of losing you will always be there, but we will ask God to give us a measure of His grace, peace, and comfort each day. We know He will provide it if only we ask.

Your journey here on Earth has ended, but now you will have endless joy in your new home in Heaven. God tells us, in His word, that He has many rooms in His mansion and that He has prepared a place for all who have accepted Him. Lindsi, we know that your name was written in the Lamb's Book of Life, and we know that you will make a joyful noise in Heaven. And though you are leaving us here on this temporal Earth, our family will all be united again in the eternal. I love you, my daughter, my princess, and God's little angel! We all love you!

Our family was also invited to a memorial service at the Children's Cancer Clinic. I was hesitant, as was the family, about attending, but we accepted the invitation. The service also recognized other children who had lost their lives. It was very emotional and touching. It was difficult to contain our feelings of pain and sadness. So many family lives are changed after a child is diagnosed with cancer. It penetrates every area of your life. Support is a must, though, not only for the patient but for the family as well. Our family was blessed to have that. Unity of the family is pivotal when battling the anxiety and uncertainty that the sickness of cancer creates. Each member needs the love and support of others as each grapples with their own personal struggles.

It was a very thoughtful gesture by the cancer clinic staff to coordinate and plan the memorial service for not only our family but many others. They wanted to remember their patients who didn't get well and to give the families the opportunity to say goodbye to them one last time. They also did not forget the families of those mourning the loss of their children. This was positive proof that the staff truly cared and desired to have a time of recognition for those lost and also to memorialize them. We are grateful for all the support and care they provided for Lindsi.

Many decisions had to be made after Lindsi's death regarding her burial. Wanda and I spent a great deal of time trying to find just the right headstone. We finally decided on one. The type of stone we selected would have to be imported from another country. The shipping time would be quite lengthy, and even more time would be needed for the engraving after its arrival to the United States. We wanted several things to be etched into the stone. We also wanted an epitaph to be added, so I began to work on it. I wanted it to be an epitaph that would fully encapsulate her life. I wanted the words to describe the wonderful person she was on this Earth and to honor her memory with those words.

My goal was to include everything that I could about Lindsi, hoping all of it would fit on the headstone. This was a daunting task, but I was ready to tackle it. There was so much that I wanted to say, in words, about her, but I knew that it would have to be limited in its length. I wound up writing a total of twenty-seven different epitaphs before settling on number twenty-eight. I was also not given a limit on the number of words for the headstone, but I felt that the words I composed captured Lindsi's life.

We sent the chosen epitaph to the monument company where we ordered the headstone. Shortly after that, the monument company contacted us and informed us that there was not enough space on the headstone for the entire epitaph. Later, someone contacted us a second time and informed us that the engraver managed to etch every word into the headstone by utilizing both sides of it. We were so happy after being told the wonderful news.

Her headstone is so beautiful. The stone has a deep pinkish hue and is shaped like a heart. The wording on it makes it even more beautiful. These words epitomize Lindsi's brief life and are a testament to our late daughter. The following is Lindsi's epitaph:

> A beautiful smile. A loving and caring heart. Amazing courage and strength. A shining light for God and a powerful legacy left for Him. An angel on earth now in Heaven. We love you and miss you.

The engraver was able to do what was, at first, an impossibility. God had other plans. God allowed those words to fit on Lindsi's headstone. He made it possible, for there is nothing impossible for Him. God displayed His omnipotence in this, and it was His plan for that entire epitaph to be etched into that small gravestone.

Wanda frequently visited Lindsi's gravesite. Her office was in town and nearby the cemetery. I worked out of town, but I think she visited Lindsi nearly every day. She would keep Lindsi's grave maintained and would change out floral arrangements, and she would, occasionally, add other items around her grave. Some items would become weathered and need replacing. I was thankful for her commitment to visit often, and I think her visits aided her in dealing with Lindsi's loss.

People react differently to loss, and they find different ways to cope with it. I think this was possibly one way that Wanda coped. However, our ultimate healer and consoler is God, and He is the one that we should lean and depend upon as we move on in our lives from day to day.

I, on the other hand, did not visit the cemetery nearly as often. It took some time for me to visit more often. It was very emotional for me to go there, as it brought back so much sadness and pain for all of her suffering and eventual death. Now, I go by there more often, and sometimes, I will tidy up around her headstone. Maybe grass needs to be pulled away from the base or dirt needs to be removed that has found its way on the marker. Solar light items or an upright floral arrangement might need to be removed and replaced, and occasionally, one or more items may need to be placed in another spot, or the base of one of the decorative displays just needs to be pushed farther into the ground for a better foundation. I want her place of memorial to look nice and clean.

Now, my visit includes one to Wanda's grave, and now, I'm the one that maintains the gravesite, which has now become two. I picked out a beautiful headstone for both of us. The color of the stone is Bahama blue. It took nearly a year for it to come and then be installed. Wanda is buried right next to Lindsi. I try to keep Wanda's gravesite tidy, as I do Lindsi's.

As I have made more trips, it has become somewhat easier. I want them to know that I miss them and that care is being taken for their temporary places of rest. Some say that time heals the wounds of losing someone, and I suppose the pain for me is not as intense as it once was, but it's still present. God is the one who provides daily comfort to lessen the pain and to handle the pain that remains.

Now, I realize that instead of anticipating sadness when visiting, it allows me to show my love and honor for them. In some small way, I can reconnect with both of them on each visit. It also calls me back to the salvation they now enjoy. Those grave markers are there as memorials to them, not their final places of rest, and those graves are not holding them, but rather, God is now holding them in His sweet embrace. I still hold both my wife and daughter in my heart for now, but one day, we will embrace again in our physical, eternal bodies, and we will forever live with God.

During each visit, I occasionally reread the epitaph I wrote for Lindsi on her headstone. It helps to remind me what a blessing it was to be her father. It also gives me so much pride to have had such an incredible daughter who touched the hearts of many. I don't hesitate to make those cemetery visits now. I can have joy for them both now, along with the sorrow.

After Lindsi's funeral, Wanda and I had to return to our jobs. I had accrued a significant amount of leave hours prior to my leave of absence to be with Lindsi and to care for her. I was able to use my sick leave hours while away from work. God had blessed me with good health, so I was able to accumulate enough leave hours to use. As my hours were reduced by the weeks off, I was already told by my department that several people would donate some of their leave if I needed it. University policy allowed for this—but only if all hours were used up.

When I returned to my position, I still had a surplus of leave and would not need any donated leave. From the point that I returned until my retirement, years later, I had acquired right around the same amount of sick leave I had at the time I left after Lindsi's sickness. This is one of those incredible blessings that God showered on me and my family. The road was long, but along the journey of Lindsi's sickness, God provided for our needs. Our needs would be many during this trial of life, but God met them.

It was quite difficult to return to our jobs, but we knew we had responsibilities for our family, and we had to continue moving forward in our lives. Our jobs were our livelihoods, so we had to get back to them. Initially, it was hard for me to focus on my job, as I was still in tremendous grief, and I'm sure that Wanda dealt with it as well, but we pushed onward as we were both dedicated to our job positions. God blessed us with our positions, and He expected us to return and be the productive workers we strived to be before Lindsi's illness.

God allowed us to become refocused on our job tasks and blessed us as we got back to work. It was so powerful to experience the things God performed in our lives. He gave us the strength and willpower to go back to our workplaces and resume our productivity as before. He renewed us each day. It's so awesome to serve a mighty God who loves us and cares about us so much.

Although I said my goodbye to Lindsi, she is still a part of my life, just as Wanda now is, and their spirits are still with me. Wonderful memories of them still remain. I think of them often with much fondness, and I was blessed to have them both in my life. I know my sons feel the same way. They had a loving and caring sister and mother.

Sometimes, I think of them and wonder about their time in Heaven and what they might be doing. I think about them watching us from Heaven and wondering if they would be pleased with the way we have proceeded forward in our lives. They can see that they have not been forgotten as well as the sadness we share in their earthly absences from us. Lindsi and Wanda are now free from all the pain and suffering and all the trials and tribulations of this world. They now bask in the incomparable and majestic beauty of the perfect place called

Heaven. They now give praise to our Heavenly Father, worship Him continually, and share a perfect existence with Him.

What joy awaits those of us who have accepted Him. That expectant joy is life eternal with Him. Our goodbyes to Lindsi were said years ago, and then to Wanda, but our hellos await us in Heaven.

Chapter 18

"ANNIVERSARY MARKERS"

With each year following Lindsi's passing comes the anniversary markers. The year 2020 would have marked her eighteenth birthday. Lindsi passed away less than two months before her tenth birthday. 2020 would have also been her senior year of high school and graduation. We had two nieces who were the same age as Lindsi, who graduated that year. Although we were happy for them, we were also saddened, at the same time, by Lindsi's absence from our lives. We didn't get to share that time with Lindsi, and it was difficult to deal with. We did have some consolation, as our church recognized Lindsi as a graduate posthumously.

Other markers come each year for Lindsi's birthdays, and the day she left us. These anniversaries bring back sorrow, but they are also times of remembrance. High school graduation and turning eighteen are one-time celebrations in a person's life.

Birthday celebrations come once a year. But think about Heaven. It's a place where there is a celebration every day for eternity. I don't know if there is such a thing as day and night in Heaven, but it is forever. What a breathtaking thought. Heaven is devoid of all the negative things that are present in this fallen world. We, as believers, can rejoice in knowing that our future home will be in Heaven, where there are no worries, stresses, or sadness. It's good to allow ourselves to think about eternal things and not be encumbered with all the evil things that are prevalent in this world. We should look upward and engage our thoughts on Heaven, where immense joy awaits. We know that there will be streets of gold, but our minds cannot comprehend or even imagine the beauty and splendor that God has created for us there.

Often, I think, about what might have been if Lindsi was still here—how tall she would be now and the color of her eyes and hair. I wonder what she would have accomplished in life and what she would look like now as an adult. I also reflect on what profession she might have chosen. Her loving and caring spirit would have possibly led her into teaching or nursing, perhaps. Becoming a missionary, either domestically or internationally, might have been her chosen field. She loved God, so it would seem logical to surmise that she may very well have considered that career. I believe that she would have excelled in whatever profession she would have chosen. But, instead of lingering on these kinds of thoughts, my focus should now remain on her salvation. She now resides where my future home will be one day, and I will be reunited with her again, along with my wife, Wanda.

I think that most people may be reluctant to mention Lindsi to me because they are just trying to be respectful and do not want to risk the possibility of upsetting me, and I can certainly understand that if that were to be the case. For me, it helps to talk about the fact that Lindsi's life meant so much to me. Talking about her to others allows me to share a testimony of the life that my little girl lived for God and the goodness of God. It also provides a way to keep Lindsi's memory alive.

I still have sweet memories to cling to and the times we shared. She injected so much joy into our lives and into the lives of others. Lindsi left a positive impact on people, and I hope those impressions lingered with them. She left indelible ones on the hearts of those she met in her lifetime. She left behind a loving legacy for people to remember. I don't hesitate to share about Lindsi in my daily conversations all these years later, when given the opportunity. It doesn't matter if it is with a friend, acquaintance, or a complete stranger. Conversing about her creates an opening to share my faith, regardless of whether that person is saved or unsaved. It not only allows me to share my personal faith, but also the faith of my daughter. We may balk or shy away from discussing spiritual matters when God puts people in our path to share our testimony, but we should not be ashamed to tell our story of redemption and about God's gift of salvation.

You may wonder how I can freely share about Lindsi without inviting all the pain and sorrow to reemerge. I will admit that it happens, especially when sharing stories that are deeply emotional for me, and it can bring tears, but I want people to know how amazing it was to witness the faith of a small child in action. Lindsi lived it out right in front of me as I had a front row seat as her earthly father, and I'm thankful that I can pass this powerful testimony on to other people I encounter. I find myself talking about Lindsi more than myself and my testimony about what God has done for me. This is, perhaps, one way that God has ordained my testimony, which is to tie in my witness of Lindsi's life from my perspective as her father with my personal testimony of His work in my life. I do acknowledge the blessings that God rendered to our family during her sickness and the blessings that He graciously continues to provide to me and my sons today.

I shared a personal testimony once with a group of men in my church at our men's prayer breakfast, which is held monthly, early in the morning before Sunday school. It was difficult for me at some points, as I shared, but God empowered me to overcome my emotions. Though I was eager to give this testimony, I also felt some anxiousness, as this was my first public testimony since Lindsi had passed away. I'm thankful for that opportunity to share at this men's prayer breakfast. I think that most of the men in attendance knew Lindsi, but it was a blessing to talk about how Lindsi lived an impactful life for God. Yes, talking about her struggles was the difficult part. The overall message recounted the goodness of my sweet daughter and how she made a difference in her life for God. This testimony had another goal as well—for the men there to take notice of the way Lindsi treated others and to encourage introspection in each of them as to how they treated others and to realize God's expectations of us, as believers.

Public speaking is not my strong suit, although I have done it a few times in my life. I can convey and articulate my thoughts more effectively through writing. I was a history major in college, so I had to write, and I had to write often. Earlier I mentioned a poem I had framed that I wrote to my wife, Wanda. Actually, I have written several poems over the years, and several of them were written for her. This is my first attempt at book writing. This endeavor, however, is a call from God. I felt His leading years ago, and it has been a long journey and process. Daily, I prayed for inspiration as I struggled to come up with more things to write about because of the brevity of Lindsi's life. I also asked God that if this was His plan and will, that this book would be published.

Lindsi's story needs to be told. I have shared some of that story verbally for years now. Her story reveals the faithfulness of a little girl, her love for God, and God's power. Throughout her life, until the end of it, God was glorified and this is one of the purposes of telling her story.

Chapter 19

"COPING WITH GRIEF"

As I type this sentence, another anniversary is quickly approaching. This year, which is now 2024, will mark twelve years since Lindsi passed from this Earth.

Many times, I have selfishly wanted her back in my presence. Too often, I let that selfish desire take hold of me, and I allow my temporal thought process to grasp me until I regain my senses and realize that God's will is perfect. It is in those moments that I fail to consider the eternal plan of God. I still cannot fully comprehend the reason God called Lindsi home, but I have accepted His plan. I had no choice or say so in the matter of Lindsi's life or death. It was totally in God's hands and in His plan. I know, deep down, that there was a purpose in His plan for Lindsi. Losing her has been tough on me and my family, but God has eased our pain and has strengthened our faith.

God's work in our terrible situation brought Him glory and recognition. His power and sovereignty were revealed. Even though God has dominion over all things and rules the universe, He still loves His creation. He shows us mercy and grace constantly. As stated earlier, I think we, as human beings, are blind, quite often, to God's wonderful blessings. He extends His mercy, grace, and love to us when experiencing trials and hardships. Even more, God grants these same things to us every moment of our lives. It's so easy to drown ourselves in our condition without any recognition of the blessings God is providing for us in those very moments. We sometimes even fail to see the blessings unfolded in times of success and prosperity. God is our true anchor for those who seek Him. God wants to hear from each one of us, and He desires for us to seek His will and to follow Him. He never walks away from us, but we often turn and walk away from Him. Remember that He is always near.

I can attest to God's faithfulness in my life. He has walked with me my whole life, but I know that I've taken small steps away from Him along the way, in my life. If we are completely honest with ourselves we have all been guilty of this, but He is always right there with us and available. God has been my rock in the good times of my life and in the difficult ones, and I can't emphasize enough the importance of God in my life and His presence—especially in my greatest times of need.

God helped me to avoid the depression that can follow a loss, and I'm so thankful for that. I have now dealt with the loss of a loved one twice in a span of just over nine years. And yes, I have suffered deep sorrow, but I often prayed to God, asking Him to keep me from falling into a deep pit of despair and hopelessness. Without Christ in my life, I don't know what state of condition I might now be in.

After Lindsi passed, our family needed to remain strong. Then, when Wanda passed, I needed to be strong for my sons, and I also needed to be a strong presence in their lives. Being away at work for all of those years caused me to be absent from home, usually five days, and, at times, six days a week during the day but Wanda was available for the boys back home and was able to meet their needs for many years. Being so far away from the family all those years with my employment was not easy but I felt that I was where God wanted me and I had full confidence in Wanda handling things at home while I was away during the day.

Logan would later attend Mississippi State, where I was employed, so that would then allow me to be there for him. Wanda had to take care of most things going on at home since her job was in our hometown, and I was an hour away with my job. Logan and Larson depended on their mother, and she did a great job attending to all of their needs.

With Wanda now gone, so many other responsibilities have fallen on me. It has been a tremendous blessing to be retired now and also be available to be there for my boys. Logan, Larson, and I have been through a lot together, and God has been gracious to us. God has enabled me to handle the tremendous load that has been placed on me now as a widower. He has been my bedrock and fortress through these turbulent times we have faced as a family. I continue to ask for daily strength from above. Along with the petition for strength, I also ask for His bestowal of wisdom to make sound decisions and those that are aligned with His will. I ask Him for His continued renewal of blessings on us, and lastly, I pray for His granting of comfort and peace for our losses.

Losing Lindsi shook me tremendously, as well as our family. It was devastating enough to witness her suffering from cancer. Her treatments and her lengthy trips to the clinic and hospital took their toll on her once-healthy body. As I have stated repeatedly, I try to blot out those horrid memories from my mind and refocus my thoughts on her inward and outward beauty before she got cancer.

We need to seek positivity and happiness in our daily lives and be thankful to God for His goodness and grace that He provides for His flock. In scripture, it tells us that if God cares for even the birds of the air, then how much more He cares for us (Matt.6:26).

I felt helpless and hopeless for some time. I needed God to remove those feelings from me. I needed to be unchained from them. I asked for Him to unburden me from my worries, pain, and sorrow. He lifted my load, enabled me, and empowered me to pick myself up and move forward again in my life.

Grief brings about these feelings and is difficult to overcome, but we must press onward. I depended on God to extract my feelings of helplessness and hopelessness, and He answered. In my heart, I knew what God desired me to do, but I also knew that what He wanted could only be made possible by my faith and trust in Him. Daily, I call upon His name to give me His peace and comfort to move forward and walk with Him. He continually fills the empty void that permeates within me. He refills that void with His love and grace.

If you are dealing with loss, do not bottle up your grief and allow it to remain, as you may open yourself up to depression. Instead, remember God and turn to Him. If you are a lost person dealing with loss, there is good news for you. Accept Jesus as your Lord and Savior. Ask Him to come into your heart. Believe, in faith, that Jesus was born on this Earth, lived as a human being, lived a sinless life, died on a cruel cross for the sins of all humanity, was resurrected on the third day after His death, and defeated death so that we, as believers, have life eternal in Heaven after we depart from this life. Only God can walk by your side in this life and never leave you. This is one of the promises of God that will never be broken.

Taking a pill or a drink from a bottle of alcohol won't help you. It may numb your feelings, but it will only be a temporary fix. A relationship with God is not temporary. It is everlasting. His love endures always as His promises. He is always present and able to ease our hurts as we continue to live our lives.

As Christians, we are not given exemptions from trials and hardships in our lifetimes. But if they visit us, we can rest in the assurance that we don't have to face it alone. We can cast all our cares, concerns, and worries onto God's throne of grace. God is omnipresent and He can shed the load of those things that encumber us. We can let go of those things by turning them over to God.

I'm so thankful for God's love for me and my family, and I thank Him for being a promise keeper, for being merciful, and for His grace that He extends to us daily. I thank Him for the gift of salvation and for carrying me through the trials of life and through the grief of losing Lindsi and, later, Wanda. And, lastly, I'm thankful for His continued presence in my life and undergirding me every day with His comfort and peace and the strength to carry on.

Many have lost loved ones all throughout history. If you have lost loved ones in the past or recently, it is my prayer that God will give each of you the comfort, peace, and strength to cope with grief and move forward in your lives. Lean on God, and depend on Him. He is there to lift you up.

There are varying periods in my life when I reflect on the passage of Lindsi. It has now been over a decade. My eyes still well up when thinking about her. I mentioned earlier about all the flowers given in her memory. I still have one of those plants to this day. This plant does not produce flower blooms. It has several names, but the one I prefer to call it is the "arrowhead plant." It is full of beautiful, deep green, and light green foliage. I have maintained and nurtured it now for many years following Lindsi's funeral. For me, it's a small reminder of her, but it also serves, somehow, as way to celebrate and honor her memory.

Just as a seed is placed into the soil to germinate and bring forth fruit, so also is that of a believer's witness to a nonbeliever. Our testimony plants a seed in the hearts of those who are lost, and then God takes over the remainder of the process. I believe that Lindsi's life and testimony sowed many seeds in the hearts of people. We came to see this through the spoken words of others. Hearing this brought us joy. Folks around our area still speak fondly of Lindsi and recall her impact for God's kingdom.

I've talked about the idea of how time heals grief and how I have felt my pain lessening over time. Again, the pain may not be as intense as before, but the pain is still present and will remain with me until my time on Earth is done and God calls me home.

My salvation gives me so much peace, and that same faith in my eternity in Heaven is linked to my faith in Lindsi and Wanda's salvation, which they now enjoy. This hope squelches out the noises of my grief and allows me to focus on my future eternity in Heaven and my reunion with loved ones.

Earlier, I talked about returning to my profession. I finally returned to my job sometime after the funeral. It may have been a couple of weeks or longer, but I knew I had to get back to my responsibilities there. It was very hard for me at first, but the busyness of my work helped me to focus on something other than my sorrow. I needed that temporary relief in order to be productive once again, to get back into some semblance of a routine in my life, and also to be the husband and father that God wanted me to be. It was still a challenge for me early on, and it was a process to work back to some state of normalcy. Our family was still shaken after the funeral, and we were still trying to pick up the fractured pieces of our lives and reconstitute ourselves. It took some time, but God ushered in His grace to make us strong enough, once again, to move forward as a family without Lindsi.

Over the years, I've had several dreams about Lindsi. In those dreams, she is alive, and she is usually healthy again. In those moments of deep sleep, I became so happy because she was with me again. Then I would awaken, and when I did, I was in a temporary state of euphoria, and I hadn't quite come to my senses yet. And then, the realization would set in. My state of mind would then rush to intense sadness. The happiness that I held during the dream and just a few moments after I awoke was quickly dissipated and replaced with sorrow. It was then that I would experience that overwhelming sense of loss all over again.

You might be wondering if I experience the same types of dreams about my wife, Wanda, and the answer is yes. My pain still resides with me. Dreams are another place in my life that produces its reappearance, but God makes a way for me to deal with it each time. I just have to go back to my faith in her salvation. Grief is one reality of life that we have to grapple with in this fallen world.

Death is inevitable for all of us, and grief is waiting in the wings to entangle those who suffer the losses of loved ones who proceed them in death, but there is good news, and that is we can call on our loving God. By calling on His name in prayer, we can ask for the gift of the Holy Spirit to comfort us. Jesus told His disciples that when He left them, He would give them the Holy Spirit to continue guiding them and to embolden them to carry on His earthly ministry. The Holy Spirit would also enable them to retain all of those things that Jesus had taught them earlier (John 14:26).

Likewise, the Holy Spirit provides us with guidance if we ask, but the gift of the third member of the Trinity gives us even more. Through the Holy Spirit, we can experience the peace of God and also the comfort that He can bring into our lives in our times of grief. The Holy Spirit also provides strength in us through the power of God.

God does not want the death of anyone to cause us to lose our hope. I've mentioned many times that after Lindsi's death, we could not give up, but only continue moving on in our lives.

God still wants us to live for Him regardless of the hardships and struggles we may go through.

When reading some stories in the Bible, we read about the losses of life, famines, and murder. All these years later, these things still occur. Sometimes, we become so fixated on our own struggles and also on the things that are going on in the world that we forget about God's providential care over everything. We sometimes see evil people get away with so much without repercussions or consequences and enjoy prosperity, but how often do we pause and recognize that God is in control. Again, we fail, at times, to grasp the bigger picture, and that is the perfect plan of God. God is also a righteous being, and regardless of the things that evil people get away with here, they will be called to judgment one day, just like the rest of us. Jesus will return and pronounce His judgment and His righteousness.

Our journey of struggles, sadness, and grief revealed something very important about God. His glory was revealed. His power and majesty were manifested in our long journey. God desires to be glorified through His people. Lindsi did not ask to be praised for her kindness and giving spirit, nor for her love for others. I believe Lindsi was the wonderful person she was because of her love for God. She was in His hands here and now, in Heaven. God accomplished great things in the life of Lindsi. Others noted it. She left a legacy of love, and she was a bright light in this dark world. Lindsi did not hide her light, but made it visible for all to see. She will always be missed and never forgotten. She forged a lasting legacy here, which was one of love and concern for others.

Many years have come and gone since her call to Heaven. Now, I am determined to keep my thoughts not on her time of illness but, instead, on her goodness, her loving kindness, and her Godly legacy. She was the most wonderful daughter that I could have ever hoped for. It is these remembrances of her and her salvation that will always chase away my sorrow.

As I continue to cope with my losses, I will also continue to seek refuge in my Heavenly Father's arms. I know He has indwelled my being with the Holy Spirit to guide my life and that He will always be there for me. I've called upon God many times in my life. He has always been a faithful friend. I can always count on Him to keep His word and to be with me always. He will never abandon His people. This is one of God's wonderful promises. I'm so thankful for this promise.

I still grieve my losses each day, and I still go through periods of sadness, especially on anniversaries that come and go. God still gives me the ability to think back on the happy times I spent with my daughter and wife. My thoughts may also carry me to their lives now in Heaven, and I can ruminate on things they might be doing at that moment. Maybe they are taking a walk through a beautiful meadow or taking a nap in the beautiful mansion rooms He made for each of them. When the pain of their absences appears, I can always go back to thinking about their happiness and joy in Heaven. Their salvation was secured when they left this Earth through the grace and mercy of our great God. They accepted Him and received the gift of salvation. His love for us is the greatest of all loves. Jesus defeated death, salvation was then made possible, and God's righteousness was justified. Those who place their trust in God will be saved and receive salvation. This salvation is freely offered to all who accept Him. So, death is not the end, but rather the beginning of our eternal life. Lindsi and Wanda are now alive with Christ. All of these things are my reasons for being at peace.

God has continually shown me His goodness, and it has sustained me in my battle with grief. Those who have suffered loss and either refuse to accept God or have never heard His word proclaimed have no genuine hope. People without God cannot create hope in themselves. How sad it is to think that those who refuse Him are missing a true gift and opportunity to experience the sovereignty and power of God. We should pray for all the lost in our world that they will hear the proclamation of God's word and that they will accept the gift that He offers to all who will acknowledge Him as their Lord and Savior.

Again, believers are not exempt or excused from hardships in life. They can appear at any time or moment. Some may not be as difficult as others, but they can still test our faith. These troubles can impact our lives, and they may endure for short or long durations after they appear. God allows these periods in life to strengthen us, and it opens up an opportunity for us to be refined and to bring us to a closer relationship with God. God desires this of every human being. He wants us to praise Him and to worship Him. God wants us to honor Him in our lives.

Some people are going to be watching how Christians handle trials in life, and some of those spectators may be non-believers. Our trial opened up an opportunity for discipleship. Though we faced the trial, our actions would indicate our relationship with Christ. I hope the way we handled our tragedy brought glory to God. I hope that if any non-believers were watching, they could see our faith in action. In our lives, our reactions to hardships might have an effect on someone who's lost.

God's power was present in our trials. His provisions were plentiful the entire time, and He met our every need. The Lord revealed His presence among us, and He infused us with His strength. He lended us support through the lives of others willing to serve Him. God lifted us up when we were downtrodden. He gave us supernatural strength for longevity to be available as caregivers. We experienced His peace and comfort. He showed us His love and mercy.

Chapter 20

"BLESSINGS"

I often think back on Lindsi's journey as we followed her. Lindsi faced many obstacles, and we faced challenges of our own. As her caregivers, Wanda and I were on constant standby.

I think Wanda was more the standby person than me. Wanda was so focused and in-tune with each of Lindsi's needs. Wanda and I had to take much time off from our professions to be Lindsi's caregiving team. I say team because we worked in tandem to make sure that every single need was met. Lindsi's needs were great, and they were many.

One of the many blessings that God provided was the availability of earned leave accumulated through my employer to be with Lindsi. I had plenty of leave built up to cover my time away from work and Wanda had the availability as she was an elected official. I have mentioned this blessing before, but I think it bears repeating because it indicates God's providence. He already had certain things in place for us before our trials were to come. To have those positions available to return to was yet another blessing.

My commutes to work were many, and they were long, over two hours a day, round trip. I logged about six hundred miles a week on those commutes, and I commuted for almost nineteen years. I occasionally think back on God's protection over all those years. I collided with two deer, head-on, I might add, and neither time did my airbags deploy. Each time, I was able to keep my vehicle on the road and continue driving. Another deer ran into the rear side of my vehicle as it crossed the road. We have a big deer population in Mississippi, so an encounter with one was not uncommon. All three deer were galloping across at full speed and came out of nowhere, it seemed.

I was also in a couple of minor accidents. One was because of a chain reaction from an unmoved vehicle at a major intersection. It was raining, and the road was slick. I braked early at the vehicle in front of me, but as I did, my car just slid, and I could not stop, so I rear-ended it. I think I was about the fourth car in the pileup. God protected me from being rear-ended by another and also from sustaining any injuries.

I was rear-ended by someone in the other accident without injury. This was another example of God's protection. I praise God for all the blessings He has provided for both me and my family all our lives.

Another facet of our time of testing involved extensive travel. This is yet another wonderful blessing to share. He provided protection during all of our long trips to the hospital, clinic, and treatment center. We had no accidents, and we never had a flat tire. We never had issues with our vehicle. At that time, we had a van, which provided plenty of room for Lindsi, space to store her wheelchair, and plenty of room for the family. We had purchased the van after we had grown to a family of five.

Another blessing came in the form of insurance coverage. Wanda and I had very good health coverage plans with our employers. Wanda also obtained a cancer policy with her position, and that coverage paid a sizeable portion of Lindsi's medical bills. God also blessed both Wanda and me with good health throughout, and this allowed us to be there for all of Lindsi's visits and to be available to care for her.

Yes, God's blessings were bountiful, and He both prepared and equipped our family for the difficult time that we were about to face.

There were many low points in our journey together. Often, that journey took us through many valleys, and the road we traveled had many twists and turns, but God navigated us all along the way. I'm thankful for the provisions He gave us. When sharing my testimony with individuals, I want them to know about Lindsi, but I also want them to know about the blessings of God. Through our weakness, God made us strong. He provided the means for Wanda and me to be there for Lindsi, to give her encouragement, to console her, and to care for her. I can't say enough about Wanda during this time. The feats that she performed can only be explained by God's presence in her life. Wanda's love for Lindsi can also be attributed to her incredible acts. We leaned on God greatly, and He answered our prayers for strength.

Every day, people are going through tough times like we experienced. Like us, they can find their strength in Him, and they can also find their hope as well in what may seem like a hopeless situation. God can grant them assurance of His presence and His comfort. They can be filled with the peace that God wrapped us with in our sorrow. God was so good to us during a terrible time in our lives. We were chosen for a time such as this, and God invested us with the tools and abilities to overcome it with His mercy and grace.

God can provide hope and assurance to others who have suffered loss as we did. They can experience the power and presence of God in times of despair and sorrow. I openly proclaim the blessings of God that He richly bestowed upon us, and each time the story of His goodness is told, God is given the glory and honor for it.

Logan was busy with sports year-round growing up. He began playing baseball around five or six with tee ball. Larson was nearing the age to begin tee ball at the time of Lindsi's sickness. With our focus shifted toward caring for Lindsi, spending time with the boys had dwindled, but we were still supportive. We would not let our situation keep them away from their endeavors. Our schedules would intertwine, but Wanda and I did our best to make it possible for at least one of us to go with the boys and get them to games and practices. I was helping coach Logan's travel baseball team, so I juggled my hours between Lindsi and the boys.

There was a time or two when neither of us could go with them. Logan was so understanding about our family situation. It hurt him to see Lindsi suffer, and he became her cheerleader. He would encourage her and spend some of the free time he had with her. We had no issues with Larson either, although he was very small at the time, but he spent time as well with Lindsi. I'm so proud of them and the great young men and sons they are to this day.

As you can see, God blessed us with three great kids. Through them being understanding, it aided us in our primary focus to remain on Lindsi. I'm so thankful for their unselfishness. At times, it felt like Wanda and I were being pulled from all directions as our family life was unraveling, but our sons made our job of parenting much easier during a very trying time.

Patience became a constant during our journey with Lindsi. More importantly, was the patience that Lindsi had to call on many times. Receiving healthcare can be very time-consuming. Wanda and I could speak to this truth as caregivers. There were those times when waiting room visits became a recurring theme. Some of the cancer clinic visits would last an entire day for Lindsi and either Wanda, me, or both of us.

There were so many other children there in need of medical attention. I will confess that Wanda was a more patient person than me, and I witnessed this in her many times. Patience is a wonderful trait to possess, and she had it. Wanda was a very selfless woman. She always put all the family's needs before her own.

I also wrote a eulogy for Wanda to be read at her funeral. It will be shared later in the book, and you will see, in this eulogy, that specialness in her. Exerting patience was a struggle for me in those waiting room periods, especially when I saw Lindsi in pain and discomfort. Her impatience was warranted because of her sickness, and mine came in those instances because it just broke my heart to see her suffering. We tried our best to make her feel better in those moments, but there was not always much that we could do to help her. Sometimes, we could find something for temporary relief.

I can't tell you how much it hurt me to see my daughter in her condition. I felt all I could do was give her encouragement and find a way to ease her constant pain. If a blood transfusion was needed, they might not have the type of blood she needed, so they would have to call it in and have it delivered, so that would require a waiting period. The transfusions, themselves, would take hours, and if her blood platelet counts were still not sufficient, then they would have to give her more.

We never knew what to expect with each visit Lindsi made to the cancer clinic. Some clinical visits resulted in hospitalizations so the call for patience was a given at every visit. This was a test for me, but God supplied me with enough patience to handle those long days. Lindsi, however, had to exert so much more patience than Wanda and me. Lindsi was in pain as she waited, not us. I know Lindsi could rarely get any rest, and our rest was limited, too. At times, the three of us were completely exhausted, but God picked us up to carry on.

Everyday life may call for patience. Some struggle with it more than others. We have a source of patience. God can calm our anxiousness to help us deal with the long waits or minor discomforts in life. We honor God by exhibiting patience as we put our faith in Him to wait. Having patience exemplifies our reliance and dependence on Him in that we put our trust in His timing for His plan to take place.

We usually have to exercise patience daily. I ask God to give me the ability to wait on His plans and not turn from Him to make my own. I'm now speaking in terms of patience for something we may ask God to do for us in our lives—not the patience of waiting to be called in for a doctor's appointment. But God wants us to be patient in those moments as well. Wanda certainly demonstrated it in her life.

There will be times in our lives requiring our patience. Technological advances may have lessened some needs for it, but situations will still come our way that will test our threshold levels. God may very well place obstacles in our path in order to draw us to Him and test our faith. He wants us to be faithful in all things and to be more like Him in our lives. We should always be faithful and humble ourselves before Him and lean on Him. God was always faithful to us before and after Lindsi's cancer was diagnosed.

Lindsi's patience, and ours, were tested daily. Our faith was also tested. Our lives were changed, but God's goodness and grace were magnified. Others saw our struggles, but they also witnessed God's power. Lindsi's incredible, although brief, life was a testimony to her faith in God. God will do all things in His timing—not on our selfish timetables. God's will cannot be changed, and His plans are infallible and perfect. He wants us to seek the will He has for each of us and find it. Faith, along with patience, are two keys to discovering it.

In our journey, God not only exhibited to us His faithfulness, but He also established His blessings for us every part of every day. The blessings I have mentioned are only a few. His blessings abound each day in our lives. We need to slow down and take a moment to give recognition to this and give God praise.

Chapter 21

"A MOTHER'S LOVE & STRENGTH"

As you can imagine or know, cancer affects the entire family. I often go back to that moment in time, sitting in that hospital waiting room for the first time and Lindsi asking me what was going to happen next. I had no definitive answer for her. How could I? Though I offered a reply to her question, I don't recall the words I spoke to her, but I'm certain that they were words to calm her. I needed to show her outward strength, but inside, I was so terrified. Her tumor diagnosis was just shocking.

I could not understand why God would allow this to happen to my sweet daughter. This was my reaction to all of this, and you are probably wondering how Wanda reacted. Well, you are about to find out. I revealed some things about my late wife earlier in the book. Now, I want to focus my attention on her for a moment.

If I were asked to describe Wanda during this time in only one word, it would be superhuman. She performed extraordinary feats while caring for Lindsi. The strength and resiliency she exhibited during that time were amazing to witness. Wanda was a bedrock in our family. She did her best to make sure that both the children's needs and mine were met.

I can't tell you how many times I saw Wanda get up from a rested position at home, the clinic, or the hospital to heed Lindsi's calls for help and assistance. If Wanda was present, she would attempt to meet her every beck and call, and if Lindsi was hospitalized or at the clinic and she could not do something for her, she would either be on her way to the nurse's desk to get a staff member to come to help her or be on the call button to alert a nurse. She was a mainstay for Lindsi. My wife was more than just a caregiver to Lindsi. She was also Lindsi's loving mother who cared so much for her and would do anything humanly possible to help her precious daughter.

I believe her amazing superhuman acts were made possible through the gifts God gave her for inner strength and resolve and the love she had for Lindsi. Wanda channeled that love for Lindsi through her efforts to be by her side almost constantly and to make sure she could successfully meet every need that was within her power .

Wanda also modeled that of a strong, Christian wife and mother who loved God and her family. I was blessed to have such a wife and mother to our children.

We received a plethora of sad reports and news along the way about Lindsi's condition, but there would also be some periodic good news received. We would rejoice in any kind of positive reports that came our way. For Lindsi to have one good day in a week was a blessing to us. That may seem like such a minor consolation, but when your daughter is suffering, any temporary relief is a blessing. We would be elated each time we heard that her platelet count was high enough for her to avoid another transfusion. This also meant that she would not have to make a long trip to the hospital to receive one.

Again, these things may seem like small blessings, but I can assure you that these meant everything to us, and we thanked

God for them. A blessing is a blessing, regardless of how significant or insignificant it might appear, because it comes from God above.

As has already been mentioned, all our trips were exhausting, but more so for Lindsi. Those trips taking her back home were the ones we looked forward to making. That meant that she would have finished a treatment, completed a transfusion, been discharged from the hospital after an infection, or that her immune system was no longer compromised. It was so much better for all of us to be back home together as a family again.

The lone trip that we did not welcome was the last one we made after being told there were no other treatment options for Lindsi. That was one of many sad days for all of us.

The label "caregiver" is used to refer to a person who takes on the responsibility for the oversight and care of another person. In our case, Wanda and I worked together as Lindsi's caregivers. To me, Wanda was the primary caregiver, and I was an assistant caregiver. Wanda stayed on top of everything so that she could provide the best care for Lindsi. She intently listened to the doctors and nurses. She asked a myriad of questions and sought to understand and be aware of all that was going on in Lindsi's medical care. The doctors even allowed us to administer medications to Lindsi so that we did not have to take her back to the clinic.

Wanda paid great attention to the instruction of the medical staff so that she could be a great caregiver. She went above and beyond to meet Lindsi's demanding needs. She clothed Lindsi, bathed her, combed her hair, and changed her, as Lindsi had to wear disposable diapers. Wanda constantly heated body wraps to place somewhere on Lindsi's hurting body. I, myself, recall using the microwave frequently to heat her wraps.

As noted before, Lindsi would constantly have to be repositioned, whether she was on the bed or on a couch. She was confined for long periods. She also had to take her medications, so this would sometimes become a dilemma as she had to swallow them. Lindsi was in a helpless state, and it was torture watching her struggle. So many times, Wanda and I had to keep our emotions in check. Wanda stayed composed every time. I did my best to prevent the tears from flowing and breaking down in front of Lindsi, and I was able to do it. I never wanted her to see me cry.

Wanda had a gentle calmness about her, and she was very patient. She met all of Lindsi's demands with great care and love. It was, at times, very uneasy to satisfy Lindsi, as her illness made things so difficult for her, but Wanda would continue to press forward by utilizing all kinds of means to find a successful solution. If one idea was unsuccessful, she would look at another plan to see if it would work. There was a continuous need for trial and error to be implemented in order to solve a new, encountered problem.

And yet, Wanda took on each challenge with such persistence. She would always give it her best effort to make Lindsi feel better. Lindsi depended on her mother so much. I'm sure the same can be said when she was a healthy and vibrant girl. There were plenty of times that Lindsi wanted me, and I always tried to be on the ready when those calls came. I was glad that I could be of assistance and have a part to play in comforting her. She meant the world to me, and I wanted to do all I could for her. Wanda felt the same way.

To this day, I am still in awe of my wife's endurance during the illness. She was dealing with sleep deprivation, for one, and she could barely take some time away to eat, much less sleep. I know that her physical and emotional health was at a low, yet she continued to go at it day after day. Lindsi rarely slept for more than a couple to a few hours at a time. Those nights in the hospital were brutal, as we were pretty much prisoners to it, like Lindsi. We would spend a week or weeks at a time there. We missed home, and I know Lindsi longed to be there.

I remember those nights when Wanda and I tried to get some rest, and a nurse would walk in at the wee hours of the morning because Lindsi had to be monitored throughout the day and night. Each time a nurse would enter, we would be awakened, but Wanda would immediately rise out of her sleep to check to see what was going on and to ask the nurse questions. At other times, Lindsi would cry out for help, and Wanda would quickly get up and be by her side to see what she needed.

For months, our lives were spent traveling to go for medical visits and spending long periods at the hospital. How sad it was for our little girl to now be living her life constantly going to doctors and spending weeks at a time in a hospital. She could no longer do the things a healthy child could do. I know it must have grieved her to no longer have an ordinary life and not to be with her friends from church and school. But I also believe that she came to the point of acceptance of her sickness, and she endured it with grace and courage.

She was special in so many ways for her whole life, not just during the period of her illness. She was so brave in her fight against cancer, and her inner strength was also revealed. I think people saw this in her life and also her relationship with God, and, in turn, it inspired them to seek a closer walk with God in their own lives. Maybe her example brought salvation to one or more lost souls. If that occurred, then praise God.

I'm so glad that my children had a wonderful mother. I'm thankful they had a mother that loved them, cared for them, and met their needs. Wanda displayed strength in weariness, calmness in adversity, and faith in hopelessness. She was a prepared believer, ready to withstand one of the darkest hours of her life and ours.

Thank you, God, for uniting us together as husband and wife and for the years we shared with each other.

Chapter 22

"PURITY OF HEART"

In the fifth chapter of the book of Matthew, Jesus is teaching His disciples. The lesson that He shared with them is called "the Beatitudes." In verse eight, Jesus tells them that those who are pure in heart are blessed and will see God (Matt. 5:8).

Lindsi displayed this quality. Her love and concern for other people were examples of her purity of the heart. That purity came from her love for her creator. It pleases God to see believers helping others, but He also wants it to spring up from an unselfish desire within us. We shouldn't expect praise for such acts, but rather, the expectation that others see our love for Christ and for the glory of God to be manifested. I never noticed a time in Lindsi's life when she had a desire to be praised or patted on the back for any of her good deeds toward other people. My story earlier about the coffee runs for teachers comes back to mind. Her thoughtfulness and desire to go the extra mile were proof of a pure heart.

Also, in the book of Mathew, chapter 5, Jesus mentions the word "light" to His disciples. He tells them they are to be lights of the world (Matt. 5:14). This command to His disciples is expected of us today. We are to be lights in the world. We live in a very dark world full of sin and death, but our witness for God will be lights that dispel the evil and wickedness in the world. Our light or witness can illuminate the pervasive darkness, and God wants our lights to shine brightly, not dimly.

In verse sixteen, Jesus tells them to let their light shine before men so that others might see their good deeds but, more importantly, that it shows praise for God through those deeds of goodness (Matt. 5:16). In Lindsi's earthly life, she was a light in this world. Her light was emitted brightly for Him. In fact, I wanted the word "light" to be included somewhere in the title of this book.

Darkness invades our lives today, as it did in biblical times. The darkness of sin, deceit, murder, blasphemy, etc., continues in our day. But even though this darkness still exists, there is also light. Jesus was the Light of the World, but we can also be this and keep it shining for God. We can claim it because Jesus instructed us to be this.

Lindsi claimed it as she took on that responsibility. As Christians, we should accept the same charge that Jesus gave to His disciples over two thousand years ago. To be that light, we must die to self and intentionally move to honor God. I will admit that I have fallen short of this many times. It is challenging to always be salt and light in the world, but we should strive to be just that. The devil is constantly waging war on our souls as he bombards us with his temptations. He will come at us from so many angles. He attempts to trap us with his cunningness. His desire for us is to do evil, not good. He will try to distort evil as good, but we must not fall prey to his deceitful traps.

If we continually recognize God's power and our reliance on Him, He will give us the power to repel the constant temptations that Satan will throw at us. He will infuse us with His wisdom to recognize right from wrong and empower us to overcome the devil and his evil intentions toward us. By doing this, we can maintain a life that is pleasing to God. We need God's Holy Spirit always to cast the devil from us each time he tries to ensnare us with his webs of deceit.

Lindsi did not allow Satan to darken her life. Even though she was going through a life-threatening illness, she still made the light within her shine for many to behold. Her light shone like that of a lighthouse beacon, and her purity of heart glorified her Heavenly Father. Her light encompassed not only our small town but also throughout the United States and abroad. God did an incredible work through a little girl in Kosciusko, Mississippi, and it truly revealed the magnificent power and sovereignty of God.

May we, as believers, be pure of heart and seek to be shining lights and honor God in all that we do. Lindsi made this cruel world brighter through her goodness. I harken back to Lindsi's phone calls to other family members. Her desire was to continue showing love and concern for someone other than herself. The pureness of her heart remained unchanged in spite of her cancer. Her illness did not affect her compassion for others. She still had that desire to serve God by serving her fellowman.

The goodness in this sweet child was phenomenal to me, and it still touches my heart. Through all of her pain and suffering, she was still thinking of others. Her life symbolized goodness, compassion, servanthood, and purity of the heart. Lindsi had run her race in this life, and she ran it well. She lived a life that modeled love and compassion for others. She claimed victory for God and left an incredible legacy that honored Him.

Chapter 23

"LINDSI'S LEGACY"

As I considered a title for this book, I thought about the legacy that Lindsi left. Her legacy was a profound one and reflected the love she had for God. She lived a life of devotion to the needs of other people. With a heart for servanthood, she brought Him glory and recognition. I can only imagine the impact she would have made for God's kingdom if she had lived into adulthood, but God's plan was for her to enter His gates to be with Him.

The questions come and go as to why God took her so soon and what more she would have contributed with a longer life. Those questions, though, stem from my temporal way of thinking. My selfish inhibitions will kick in, and I will start to feel that strong desire for Lindsi to still be with us, but the reality is that God is omniscient, and His plans will be carried out perfectly.

It is so hard for us to see how God's plans are perfect when they bring us sorrow and grief. But somehow, His plans are for good. For us, these plans make no sense, but for God, they are plans that will always work for His glory. As I have grieved my losses for years now, I have come to the point of acceptance of God's plans for my wife and daughter. God used both my daughter and my wife in special ways, as they left spiritual imprints of their relationship with God. And they also received their rewards of salvation.

Through faith, I hold that they now enjoy the eternal bliss of perfection in Heaven. I think His plans and all the mysteries of the earth and universe will be fully disclosed to us when we, as believers, are called to our eternal home.

Lindsi was a wonderful human being in every way. She gave so much of herself to those around her, and she enhanced their lives. She availed herself to be used by God to meet the needs of others in her life. I think about the parable of the Good Samaritan and the lengths to which he provided assistance to a traveler who was beaten and robbed (Luke 10:30-35). Lindsi put others' needs before her own, and her actions confirmed this. Her unselfishness could not be more greatly illustrated than by the story I have already partly shared.

Lindsi could stay at home at different times when her blood counts remained at sufficient levels, giving ample strength to her immune system. I was at home with her one particular day, and she was lying on a couch in the living room. She asked for the phone to be put by her. Well, she picked up that phone and began calling several family members to check on them. She wanted to make sure that they were okay. Lindsi did this out of her own volition and she was doing so in her terrible condition, and she would do this for days.

Of course, we received many calls asking how she felt, and she would get on the phone with them and talk away. I'm sure, on those calls, that she was asking if they were okay. That was who Lindsi was, a sweet, caring, and loving child. For Lindsi, in her state of suffering, to be concerned about others is so amazing.

On top of that is the fact that she was just a child. I think most children at this age would be selfish, mostly, and only concerned about themselves, but I could see God's goodness magnified and flowing through Lindsi. I could sense the love and strong relationship she shared with God above. He was using Lindsi to minister to others, even in her dire illness. She was giving glory to God and bringing Him such honor.

All that Lindsi had in her earthly life was left behind. Any accomplishments she achieved, awards received, or material possessions owned stayed here. Sure, these things can be counted as mementos for those of us Lindsi left behind, but they pale, in comparison, to the legacy she built here. Her mark left in this world was pleasing to God. Other than her salvation, it was her legacy that mattered to God. Her legacy influenced lives for Him.

Again, I was so blessed to be chosen by God to be Lindsi's father and to see God's mighty hand on her and the work she accomplished for Him and through Him. We should seek to leave a legacy of goodness when we depart from this earth, a legacy for God.

I currently serve as a Sunday school teacher for an older adult men's class. This age group is around 70 to mid-70s. I am still in my 50s, so there is a slight age gap, but it has been a blessing to be a part of this group. Before teaching this class, I taught an 80- year-old and up men's class. In prior years, I have taught a 7th-grade boy's class, a college class, and other adult classes. I'm also an ordained deacon. It has been an honor to be called by God to serve Him in these positions of the church.

I recently recalled a lesson from my current class. This lesson centered on the pending death of Moses on Mount Nebo. Moses had led the Israelites for many years. As Moses and the Israelites neared the promised land of Canaan, God told Moses that He would not enter it. He asked Him to climb up Mount Nebo to view the land that He would not set foot in. Moses went to be with God on that mountain (Deut. 36:1-6).

So, the question was raised about the legacies that people leave after their deaths. What will be said of us after we die?

It is a profound question—and one to ponder upon. I go back to Lindsi's legacy. Hers was a powerful one. Her short life was fruitful and one that probably still resonates with people to this very day. I hope that it has done so.

Now, that is the kind of legacy we should long to leave in this world. Lindsi's longing to help others was real. Her servanthood was genuine, and she expected nothing in return for her outpouring of love for others. Lindsi's legacy might continue to transform the way others live. Her life and death opened up the eyes of those she touched. She sowed seeds for God here, and maybe lives were saved and lives changed as a result.

Another part of Lindsi's epitaph mentions her enduring legacy. That legacy was full of love and concern for humankind. She was called for a purpose, and she fulfilled it. Each of us has a calling and purpose in our lives. To be used by God requires faith and willingness. We also need to pray, asking Him to guide us to follow His will for us and for wisdom to make the choices He wants us to make. We also need to be committed to what God calls us to do.

All of us are called to be witnesses to the lost. We need God's emboldenment to go out and share our testimony with those who are lost. The lost should see something different in us and the way we live our lives. In turn, the lost will see the joy and peace we have in our relationship with God, and they will want to experience that and, hopefully, accept Him. If we can accomplish this, we contribute to the work of building God's kingdom. You don't have to become a missionary, an evangelist, etc., but only be willing to tell others about Christ. You may have heard the saying about God not calling the equipped but rather equipping those He has called. God will make provisions for us in our witnessing. His Holy Spirit will guide us.

Lindsi heeded God's call. She remained faithful even in the face of her battle with cancer. Lindsi's faith was made perfect in Him. She was used in a special way to minister to those who might not have known God.

Lindsi had a physical illness. Lost people have a spiritual sickness. God still used Lindsi, in her physically sick condition, to impact those suffering from spiritual sickness. In turn, Lindsi's physical sickness was healed by God's grace upon her death and her salvation. She won the victory over death by the blood of Jesus. It is amazing to see the works that God can do through those who believe in Him. Lindsi's legacy was forged, and it fulfilled God's plan before He called her to Heaven.

I devoted an earlier chapter to mementos. Lindsi left us a memento, and it was her lasting legacy. Lindsi loved her Savior and extended her love for Him out to others. Her actions were evidence of her love for God. We should make that effort to extend love for people by showing compassion and concern. After we have left this earth and people look back on our lives, what will they say of us? What will their memories be of us? What type of legacy did we leave? Was it a legacy that pleased God? I believe that Lindsi's legacy did so.

As has been said, this book has been years in the making. Sporadic writings have traversed the years. Lindsi's life was brief, so writing became problematic after the initial stages of the manuscript, but I felt God's call to continue with this pursuit. I prayed for His inspiration often to continue with my writing. There would be lapses along the way as I struggled to continue coming up with more subjects to write about Lindsi. I will have more to say about this later.

As you have read thus far, many things have transpired over the years. My family has experienced so much sorrow and grief. Writing about Lindsi has been good for me, even with the revisitation of her sickness and the tears shed. But I can honestly say that it has been a labor of love. I wanted to tell Lindsi's story to people in a book, and I hope that many will read her story. Her darkest hours fighting cancer had to be retold, as it was part of her life, and I think it's a remarkable testimony to be shared. We made that journey with Lindsi, too. This journey was fraught with deep valleys of sorrow and pits of despair, along with uncertainty and hopelessness.

The good news is that God brought all of us through it, and He is still with us today. He lifted our spirits from despair, gave us hope when we felt hopeless, provided us joy in our sorrow, and granted us peace in our uncertainty. We completed the journey with Lindsi, with God by our side.

I love you, Lindsi, my sweet princess! I love you, Wanda, my amazing wife! We miss you both dearly and will see you again in Heaven eternal. All glory and honor to our Heavenly Father.

EPILOGUE

I began working on a manuscript for this book ten years ago. Lindsi passed away on March 10th, 2012. Again, writing was very intermittent for me over the past ten years. I worked full-time for most of these years; plus, I was commuting to work five days a week, and the commutes were long. As I had stated earlier, I did this for almost nineteen years, so my work employment took up a lot of time in my life. I had other state employment jobs prior to this last one. One of the other positions was in the town we lived in. I was then blessed to be offered a position at Mississippi State University, where I retired. The position required the commute as my wife, Wanda, was an elected county official, and this required us to reside in the county that she served.

I have been retired for three years now. When I retired, I completed just over twenty-six years of service credit as a state employee. I was blessed to be able to retire at a fairly young age. Wanda was almost four years younger than me. She would have been eligible to retire at an even younger age than me. She was serving her fifth term as the circuit clerk of our county. I was excited that we could both be retired together in a few more years. Then, suddenly, our family was struck by yet another tragedy.

On September 1st, 2021, my wife of nearly twenty-five years passed away from the Covid-19 virus. Wanda was just fifty-one years old. Prior to her sickness, she was in good health and had no underlying conditions.

We contracted the virus at the same time. We made appointments to see a doctor soon after we became ill. Upon our arrival, we were both given swab tests. At this time, patients could not enter the clinic because of the pandemic, so all of this was done from our vehicle. After the tests were administered, we were told to wait in the parking lot for the test results. Wanda's test came back positive for the virus, but my initial test was negative. Since I was exhibiting symptoms, they wanted to perform another swab test on me. I understood them to say that this secondary test would be sent off to another lab, and they would provide the test results to me later. Well, I never heard back from the clinic, so I started calling them, trying to find out the test results. After calling for the second or third time, they finally told me I was positive for the virus.

In the meantime, Wanda and I would have to remain at home and quarantine. After my late finding, I would have to take more precautions with quarantining. Wanda's condition quickly worsened. The virus hit me hard as well, but my condition was not as severe as hers. I had taken a single shot Covid vaccine earlier in March of that year, but Wanda had not been vaccinated, as she refused to do so. Honestly, I didn't want to get this vaccination either, but I was working on a college campus, and the pandemic was so widespread, so I went ahead and took it. I also encouraged Wanda to get one since her office was constantly busy with people, but she absolutely refused to get one. I must admit, I sometimes wonder if Wanda would still be here today if she had been vaccinated.

Now, we were stuck at home with this sickness. Soon, Wanda could barely get up and walk, and her breathing was in decline. Within the next day or two, we received a phone call from either the clinic or the hospital. The person told me they could see Wanda, but it would be another day or two. Apparently, Wanda had texted someone at the clinic. It was difficult for Wanda to communicate with me, as she was struggling to talk so I was not aware of her earlier correspondence. Wanda's breathing was becoming more difficult. I was still very ill but could still function somewhat.

Also, I was supposed to stay away from Wanda, but she needed my help. So, I assisted her as much as I could while also trying to keep some distance between us. I knew she needed much more attention than me, so I did what I could do for her.

The time came for her appointment, but I was told to take her to the hospital. As I helped Wanda get ready, I soon realized that she was really struggling to breathe. I did not know how severe it had become because I tried to keep as much distance as I could as I helped her. As we exited the car, there was a rather lengthy walk to the hospital doors. I had to hold her upright to get her there, and I knew she was in serious condition.

After we entered, she was told to go up to the second floor of the hospital. They then told me I could not go any farther with Wanda. She would have to take even more steps to get to the elevator doors on her own. Looking back, I don't know why I didn't demand a wheelchair for her, but that probably would have necessitated more waiting, and she needed attention immediately. I stood there at the desk and watched helplessly as she struggled to make her way to the elevator. I was struck with fear and uncertainty again, like that experienced with Lindsi.

I went home after leaving the hospital. I frantically waited to get word from Wanda or the hospital. Later, I received a text from Wanda. In it, she said that it was too late for them to utilize infusion therapy. This procedure has been effective with some Covid-19 patients. Unfortunately, her condition had deteriorated to such a critical level that this procedure would not be effective. She had to be put on oxygen soon after her admittance.

Then, later that night, in the wee hours of the morning, I received a call from the doctor on-call at the hospital. His news was grim. He told me that Wanda needed to be transferred to another hospital immediately, where she could be put in an intensive care unit. Our state was inundated with COVID-19 patients at that time, and they were desperately searching for a hospital with an ICU bed. They were soon able to find another hospital about an hour away.

At that point, I was full of anxiety, as there was nothing I could do for Wanda other than to pray and wait for more news. They told me the name of the hospital where she would be transported, but I couldn't see her. Larson, my youngest son, was still in high school, and Logan, my oldest son, was in college. I, of course, was still dealing with my sickness as well as having to quarantine, but I also needed to be at home for them, so I had no choice but to remain at home.

The phone rang daily from others concerned, and I would do the best I could to keep them informed from the information I had gleaned from the new hospital. Helplessness and fear gripped me again. The pain of the past was happening all over again in my life. First, it was my precious daughter and now, my wife and helpmate.

I would call daily for updates, and sometimes, they would call me. I would talk to different nurses along the way, as they would change shifts each day. Some days seemed hopeful, with encouraging news from the staff. Then, other days were disheartening, as I was told of setbacks. Wanda had to wear an oxygen mask constantly, and it had to be fitted tightly to prevent any oxygen from escaping.

The staff told me later that Wanda had attempted to remove her mask as she struggled to keep wearing it. Hearing that just crushed me. How awful to have to suffer wearing a device for as long as she had. They would periodically remove her mask to see if her oxygen levels would remain steady. Each time they tried it, her oxygen levels would quickly drop. I was eventually told by the medical staff that if they didn't call me, Wanda was okay, but if they did call, her condition had worsened.

So, each day, I prayed the phone wouldn't ring. When they did call, I knew it was them because they called me on our home phone, which had caller ID. Taking those calls was excruciating, and my heart raced as I answered them. And some of those incoming calls were not reports of her condition, but only requests for some information they needed about Wanda.

My days consisted of taking care of things at home and waiting for phone calls. I was experiencing another time in my life—one of hopelessness, angst, and worry. I wanted to hear the news of improvement and a timetable of when she could return home.

My thought process was that I would handle everything but that it would only be temporary, and Wanda would be back home soon, and everything would be back to normal. With me away at work for all of those years, Wanda was strapped with most of the responsibilities at home. She was busy with work but also tending to all the needs of our sons. She took care of things inside the household as well, but I handled the outside work over those years that I was working away from home.

Wanda was very active in our church and served on many committees and also served as the treasurer for the high school athletic booster club for every sport for years. After her death, two signs were placed in her memory at the Kosciusko High School baseball field. One was affixed to the outfield fence, and a smaller one was placed indirectly behind the backstop on the third-base side. It was positioned right in front of the seats where Wanda and I sat watching Larson play.

She also handled all our finances. With her absence, I was now responsible for everything here. I was not a stranger to the kitchen or the utility room. During our years of marriage, I would help Wanda with different household chores, and I would cook meals for the family occasionally, but handling the finances was something that I was not acquainted with, as I had not been involved in this area for years. Wanda and

I shared some of this responsibility earlier on in our marriage, but eventually, she took over completely.

With her away, all of this was now thrust upon me. Bills had to be paid, but I was not aware of what needed to be paid or what had already been paid for the month. It was a challenging undertaking and very overwhelming, but I got things under control, and I thank God for His wisdom.

Again, I thought that this would only last for a short duration. I would just need to keep things in order until Wanda got well and came back home. I wanted everything to be just right when she returned.

The last time I saw Wanda standing was when she made her entry through the elevator doors at the hospital. I wanted to be able to see her soon, but I was not permitted to due to the pandemic restrictions and her confinement in the ICU. One of the last text messages that I recall from Wanda was the one sent when she was at our hospital before being transported. I may have gotten a couple more texts, but the memories are blurry now. I would send numerous texts later without replies.

I would make several calls to the other hospital, especially when the texts stopped coming. I was told that her phone was probably dead and had not been charged back up. I guess this gave me a little relief, but I just wanted to hear her voice again and be able to talk to her. I wanted to give her encouragement and tell her how much I loved her, and I wanted her to come back home to me and our sons.

To hear from her would have meant so much. I tried to wait patiently in the expectation that she would eventually call or text me. Then, later, my cell phone rang. I didn't know the person calling me, but it was a FaceTime call. I took the call, and suddenly, I saw Wanda. She was lying on a bed with an oxygen mask. I was so excited to see her, but when she saw me, she suddenly burst into tears.

Somehow, I was able to restrain my emotions. I told her I loved her, that we missed her dearly, and that we wanted her to be back home with us. I told her to be strong and to continue fighting to get better. I also told her that everything was fine at home and that I was taking care of things.

Wanda could not communicate, as the mask constricted her speech, in addition to her difficulty with breathing. It was soon revealed that the call came from a cell phone owned by one of the hospital nurses who was on call, and she was responsible for connecting us. I was so grateful for that nurse and her thoughtfulness.

Although it was very difficult to watch my beautiful wife suffer, I got the opportunity to see her again and reconnect with her. I hope she could hear every word I spoke to her.

I was later told that Wanda would be put on a ventilator. Earlier, I had heard that some patients with acute respiratory infections from the virus would need ventilators, as they could no longer breathe on their own. Needing to be put on a ventilator to breathe was and is very serious, as it is the last option for patients with respiratory illnesses.

I still held out hope that her condition would improve. I prayed daily for healing to take place. God could heal her in His power if He willed it. With each passing day, I was filled with such heaviness and dread. I fell into that same state of helplessness that I experienced years earlier. I asked for God to ease Wanda's struggles and to bring her back home to me.

Sometime later, an encouraging call came. An incoming call flashed on my cell phone. I did not know who the caller was, but I answered the phone. If I recall correctly, she was not a hospital staff person, per se, but some type of social worker. She was calling to give me some potentially positive news. She told me that Wanda was improving and that if she continued to make progress, they would make plans to move her to a rehab facility, where she could receive therapy for any damage caused by being on the ventilator.

The social worker said it was possible that Wanda would have some brain damage, and she might also have sustained some physical disabilities that would have to be addressed with therapy. Still, this news lifted my spirits, and I became more hopeful that God had performed the miracle that I had prayed for, but more time was needed to make sure she had made a turn. I had been on bended knees at my bedside, praying often for another miracle. I had prayed similar ones for a miracle in Lindsi years earlier.

I needed patience for the waiting and God's peace to replace the worry and anxiety I was experiencing. Maybe a day after the hopeful report, the medical staff called me. Wanda had taken a turn for the worse now. I just couldn't understand this. One day, I was told that Wanda may be leaving the ICU and then the hospital, to now being back on a ventilator. The news quickly dashed my hopes.

I was on an emotional roller-coaster, going from one extreme to another, where my lows went to highness, then back to lowness. Although my hopes had faded, I would not stop praying.

I won't forget that last call from the hospital. Oh, how I dreaded every call from them. This call was a devastating blow to me. Once before, I was shaken to my core when a group of doctors told me there were no other alternatives to save Lindsi's life, and now Wanda had no other alternatives to help her get well. I was told that my wife did not have much longer to live.

I lost my dear daughter, and now I was about to lose my wife. My heart was broken for a second time. I had picked up the pieces nine years ago and moved on in life, and now I was about to suffer another loss.

I was told that Wanda would probably not make it through the night. We made our way to the hospital later that day. The drive down to the hospital was so somber. I was reliving the nightmare of losing someone so close to me.

We arrived about an hour later and made our way into the hospital waiting room. I remember our faithful pastor being there with us to provide comforting words in our grief. We had been in the waiting room for some time. Then, someone from the medical staff approached us and told us we could go inside the ICU room to sit with Wanda.

I was a little hesitant at first, as there were more Covid patients in that area that were near death. I also had some apprehension because of the threat of the contagion, but I wanted to see Wanda one last time. Logan, Larson, and I were allowed to all go in together, and Wanda's parents were allowed in as well. I knew that their grief was great like mine, as they were losing a wonderful daughter.

All of us had to put on protective suits before entering. Wanda was not conscious. We just loved on her and talked to her for hours. I sat by her side and made the most of that time with her. Thinking back, I hope she could hear our voices and know we were there to be with her. I'm thankful that we could see her one more time before she went to be with God. I told my boys that this would be our final goodbye to Wanda, and they agreed.

As we made our way back home, the reality set in that the life of our family would be altered yet again. Logan and Larson would soon become motherless, and I would lose my wife. We had to bear grief once more. On that drive home, I told my boys that we had to stay strong and move forward. I told them we were still a family. I also told them I loved them, that God was going to take care of us, and that we would be okay.

My hopes of Wanda's return were obliterated. I had been retired from state service for only a few months and was enjoying a period of being back home again with the family, and Wanda and I had some planning to do together about our future, but now, I would have to make entirely different ones without her. However, there would be one final decision we would make together before she left this earth. I want to share that story with you now.

I had plans to reenter the workforce at some point and applied for a part-time position not long after my retirement. Later, I received a call about this position, and the employer wanted to see if I was still interested in interviewing for it.

Wanda was hospitalized at the time. I had recovered from Covid but was left with its lingering effects. The virus had left me with no taste, loss of normal smelling senses, and brain fog. The lack of the sense of smell stayed with me for over a year. During that time, my only sense of smell was awful. I had read that the scents of COVID victims varied. For me, everything smelled bad, like that of skunk spray. I'm not sure, to this day, if my smell is as heightened as it once was. My sense of taste has finally returned. I think my memory may have been slightly affected by the virus, but it may also be a combination of getting older, too.

Upon the offer of an interview, I was conflicted. At that point in time, my focus was on Wanda and her condition. This interview offer was now secondary to me. I needed and wanted to continue taking care of business and other important matters at home, but I also needed to secure a new job. What was I to do? Should I interview for the job or decline it?

At first, I gave it some thought, and I feel sure that I prayed about it as well, and then the answer came to me. I knew what I needed to do, so I made my next move. I would contact Wanda, tell her about the opportunity, and then ask for her opinion as to what I should do.

We had made many important decisions together as husband and wife, and I was not going to make this one without her input. I valued her opinion on this. But there might be a potential problem, since our communication with each other was very limited. I wasn't sure if I would ever get a response, but I wanted to get her answer before I made my decision.

I sent her the text, and by the grace of God, I got a reply from her. She told me in that text that she wanted me to go through with that interview and that I was not to worry about her. Her answer confirmed the decision I would make. I interviewed for that position. They offered me the job, I think, the very next day after the interview. For me, the offer was bittersweet. Yes, I was happy to be selected, but I was also in sorrow for my wife, fighting for her life.

I told my future employer about my situation. They were very understanding and made accommodations for me to begin my employment at a later date. That date came much later as Wanda passed away, and I had so much to deal with, including handling my grief.

I finally reached a point to move on, and I let my new employer know I was ready to start, or so I thought. This new position would require more commuting for me, but not as long as my old one required. I felt miserable from the time I got out of bed, left to go to work until I got back home. After just one day, I resigned.

I felt like God was telling me I was not where I needed to be, but that being at home for my family was that place. God had already set His plan in motion and had all of His provisions in place for me and my boys. We were eligible to receive survivor benefits from Wanda's retirement, along with my retirement income. This allowed me to remain at home and take care of the many issues that needed attention. And they were numerous. There are many issues to deal with after losing a spouse. This is yet another example of God's goodness and grace.

Wanda did not pass away that night, but sometime the next day. When I found out that she had not yet passed, I decided

I would not go back. The pain would have been too great. One nurse on-call that night talked at length to me. In our conversation, he told me it would be an unpleasant sight, as Wanda was nearing death. That nurse also shared with me that if Wanda had gotten off the ventilator and eventually made it back home, she would probably have had to use an oxygen tank for the rest of her life, and she would have suffered brain damage and would no longer live a normal life.

I wanted Lindsi's pain to end. I didn't want to lose her, but I didn't want her to suffer any longer, either. If what the nurse said was true, I wouldn't have wanted Wanda to struggle the rest of her natural life, but I certainly didn't want to lose her as well. I lay by my sweet Lindsi's side until her death. I did not want to go through the experience of watching a loved one die again. To go through that again would have been too much for me.

My grief began when I got that phone call. The pain of losing them is still with me, but I can tell you that when I think about their eternity in Heaven now, joy fills my soul, and a calming peace embraces me. Their earthly sicknesses were eradicated forever, and they now have perfected bodies. Yes, I still ache from their physical absences, but I also retain happiness for their salvation. Our family will be reunited again in Heaven one day.

I have shared the eulogy that I wrote for Lindsi. I now want to share the eulogy that I wrote for Wanda. Our church pastor read her eulogy at her funeral service at my request. He had also read Lindsi's eulogy. As you read it, I think you will see similarities between Wanda and Lindsi. Both had the heart of a servant. This is Wanda's eulogy in its entirety:

Wanda: A Tribute To My Wife

Where do I begin? There are so many places to start. I'll go back about ten years ago. Our sweet daughter, Lindsi, was diagnosed with a rare brain tumor. Some mothers might have crumbled at the news, but not you. Instead, you were an immovable object. You were at her side constantly all day and night to try to meet every need that Lindsi had.

You were the bedrock of our family. The actions you displayed all that time appeared superhuman to me, but I know that God granted it to you, but you had to be willing to do it. I greatly appreciated and admired all that you gave of yourself to Lindsi, and that was your love, care, and concern for our little girl. I know that you and I were Lindsi's caregivers, but you were truly that and more to her. You were amazing through all of it.

My next destination in this tribute to you was your unselfishness. You not only exhibited this wonderful trait during Lindsi's sickness, but also in the lives of our family. I don't know how many times we would go to a store, and you would make a direct route to the children's clothes section to start looking at clothing for the kids. Then you might escort me to the men's section. Rarely did you ever buy yourself anything, much less go to look at something for yourself. Sometimes, you would bring me an item from the store that you thought I might like or something I may have asked you to get me earlier.

You always put our needs ahead of yours, and you were willing to spend all that time helping us to find something at the expense of doing without for yourself. You would always strive to meet the needs of all our children and myself. Don't think I did not notice it. I have never forgotten that about you, sweetheart.

Your support for the children was incredible. You spent hours washing baseball uniforms and making sure each one had a clean one to wear the next day or the next game. You traveled many miles over the years to support them, whether it be a baseball tournament the boys were playing in or a dance competition with Lindsi. You rarely missed a game or event. You sacrificed so much of your time to be there for them. I know that you loved them very much. Your support for them was one of the many ways you showed that love for each of them.

Next location would be your servanthood. Not only for your service to the people of Attala county as Circuit Clerk but also your service to the community and to our church. You dedicated your working career of over thirty years to the Circuit Clerk's office as both a Deputy Circuit Clerk and then as Circuit Clerk, serving your fifth consecutive term in office. You also served many years as secretary of the KHS Booster Club and handling all the accounts of multiple sports teams. You were dedicated to serving our church. You served on numerous church committees, some with me, and teaching children's Bible classes on Sunday night. You were always willing to serve God and always faithful to attend church.

You were a godly woman, and you sought to please Him in all the things you did in church. Thank you for instilling Christian values in our children. You were also a person of your word. I could always depend and rely upon you for things, and you did it so well, and you have my admiration for it.

So, now for my last stop. You were a wonderful wife and mother to our three children. You loved on them and always made sure they wanted for nothing. I did appreciate the fact that you would have them run some things by me before decisions were made. At times, I felt like I was the villain because I would not always say "yes." And, sometimes, you may have said "yes" before sending them to me with my "no" reply, but thanks for still sending them to me to get my answer.

I just wanted to add a little levity today because even with the sorrow of your absence now, it is a joy that you have entered Heaven through God's free gift of salvation.

And now, we are at the final destination of your tribute. You were a wonderful wife to me for all the things that have been mentioned. You were my best friend and helpmate. God gave us over twenty-four years together, and we almost made it to number twenty-five next May. I was honored and blessed to be your husband, and I will greatly miss you and the wonderful times and milestones we shared together. I thank God for the years of marriage we enjoyed.

I told you this at the hospital, and I hope my words reached you—and that is, that I love you, and I always will love you. And you know that Logan and Larson love and miss you, and Lindsi has her wonderful mother with her again.

We will be okay down here for now as we still have each other, and all three of us are going to remain strong as a family because of our love for each other, our love for you, and the love of our Heavenly Father. We all love you and Lindsi very much and rejoice for you both in Heaven and your reunion. Our comfort is in our faith in God that we will all be reunited again as a family in Heaven.

Your loving husband and sons,

Tim, Logan, and Larson

Lindsi and Wanda definitely shared some similar character traits. They lived their lives with purpose. They looked beyond their own needs to satisfy the needs of someone else. Both lives made a difference in this world. They made it better for me, for Logan, for Larson, and for many others. I'm so blessed that they came into my life and for the times we shared. I wanted it to last for a lifetime, but that was not my choice to make. It was the will of God. Our time on this earth is fleeting, but the good times shared with those we love are a blessing from God, no matter the duration. I enjoyed the precious nine years I had with Lindsi and over twenty-five years with Wanda. What joy it brings to me when I think about our reunion in eternity. There, no more goodbyes will have to be said.

Writing this book has been a long and arduous one. Honestly, months and months would pass by and no words were written. My once strong inclination to write would become an afterthought. There are valid reasons this happened, and I have already shared most of them. My work career took up much of my time each week.

When the Covid pandemic worsened, I worked remotely from home. This lasted for some time but only accounted for a minute period in the years since I felt compelled to begin writing. I have shared with you some things about Logan and Larson and their busy lives playing sports. Sports competitions and practices stretched out our schedules, and spending some quality time at home was almost nonexistent. It seemed that sports lasted nearly all year long with very little downtime. By the time Logan was moved to the varsity baseball team after completing just one season of junior high baseball as a 7th grader, he was committed to the game of baseball. The same could be said of Larson, as his focus became baseball as he entered his 7th-grade year of junior high school.

Aside from their baseball commitments to their school, they would also play it during the summer. Both of them played showcase baseball later on, after regular travel baseball. The showcases they played in required extensive travel. They played some in Atlanta, which were our longest trips. These tournaments took up our weekends as well. I tried to be there for every game, but that was not always possible because of work commitments and my time as one of Lindsi's caregivers. Wanda and I were pulled to and fro, but we wanted to always be supportive parents. For the boys, it was baseball, and it became a year-round commitment for them. So far, these reasons have centered on my work responsibilities and my family commitments, but there were other issues involved that played a role in my writing lapses.

There were periods in this timeline that I would write frequently. But, so many times, my busyness in life caused me to forget about writing, and I would go for months at a time without even a thought about it. My commitment to writing often took a backseat. Then, there would be times when I experienced writer's block. I've never taken a course specifically on book writing. However, I completed a particular course in college called Historiography and Historical Methods. I mentioned earlier that I earned a degree in history. This course was a required one for my major. It was an intensive writing course, and it required a lengthy paper to be written and turned in at the end of the semester. The work on that paper demanded many hours for completion. So, writing, in itself, was not foreign to me.

I've penned a few poems over the years as well. But to write about my own daughter and her life was very challenging, to a point. I say to a point because of three things. One, my memories had become hazy as to the succession of the events of Lindsi's sickness. I couldn't recall the exact details of the cancer illness timeline. Two was Lindsi's brevity of life, and this made it difficult to become a full-blown wordsmith. I don't know if this is a writing method, but I would liken it to brainstorming. Aside from the overall story of Lindsi's battle, finding other themes to write about became more trying, so I decided to sit down and compile a list of things to write about. Initially, I was able to come up with a few subject themes. From there, I would start writing paragraphs on each one. If another subject theme came to mind, I would return to that list and write it down.

As the pages mounted, that list began to shrink as I would mark off a subject once I was satisfied that I had written an ample number of pages which brings me to my third reason. I was running out of things to write about. At the outset, I felt God's call to at least put words to paper about Lindsi's life, regardless if it ever got published. At a later point, it became more and more cumbersome to come up with subject areas to write about. I needed more ideas. To do so, I would need God's inspiration, and I wanted this writing to be inspired by Him. So, I prayed daily for that inspiration to come as I continued my work.

At the beginning of 2024, I made it a priority to resume writing on the manuscript with the goal of achieving its completion. So, I put a notification alert on my phone to remind me each day to work on the manuscript. I set it to continue every day at that point, and it reminded me to remain fully focused and fully committed to its conclusion. That message reminder would pop up on my phone all throughout the day and night. Once I turned that notification alert on, I began working nearly every day on it for over a month or longer. I would also work on the manuscript for almost entire days with a break here and there to eat a meal and then carry on into late night hours. I was determined to see this manuscript through. Sometimes, I felt both physically and mentally exhausted, but I made this a priority. It was my goal to complete the manuscript and continue to follow God's lead.

Finally, I reached that point of concluding my writings, or so I thought. You see, after I placed that last legal pad page on that tall stack of periodic writings, my work was not done. Now, I had to go back through that mound of collected writings and sort it all out into a cohesive story. This process took me a week or two to complete. As I worked toward organizing my writings into some semblance of a book, I began writing even more and renaming title pages. This was not an easy thing to do, but God gave me guidance.

After I lost Wanda, I became a single parent, but looking back on it, I really became one when she entered that hospital. My life changed dramatically. I had been taking care of those things at home while Wanda was away, but now, I would face more challenges that come with the loss of a spouse. Some of my days were spent at the kitchen table with a phone in my hand, attempting to take care of so many things that needed to be changed. I would be on the phone for hours at a time. It was overwhelming and exhausting, but God helped me to persevere. Sometimes, I thought the worst had been overcome, and then another obstacle would appear, but gradually, more and more things would be taken care of, and life seemed to get back to some degree of normalcy. God brought me through that time of change.

It has been nearly three years now since Wanda's death. I have endured much grief over the years, as my sons have. We have remained resilient, and we are still a strong family unit. Through all the sorrow, I can testify to this. God is so good. When I reflect on these tragic times, I remember the blessings of God. He has showered my family and me with so many of them. He brought me and my sons through very difficult times.

So much has changed for us. Logan is engaged to be married soon, and Larson is attending college now. I know it has been hard for them, but they have handled their adversities so well, and I'm so proud of them and how they have continued to press on in each of their lives. I think about Larson playing two of his last high school seasons of baseball, attending school, and then graduating high school without his mother being there. She did so much for Larson, like Logan, and she was always there for them when they needed her. I know they will never forget her and will always keep her near and dear in their hearts. For me, the same can be said. I miss my two girls very much. I think we honor them both by remaining strong and moving on in our lives.

This book was conceived as a dedication to Lindsi and God. Given the circumstances now, this book is also dedicated to my loving wife, Wanda. The lives of my daughter and my wife are to be commended. They were two of my blessings and joys in life. They were loved, and they are loved today. Losing them was so painful and heartbreaking. I never thought that I would outlive my daughter. I never thought about outliving my wife. Their losses still bring us sadness. They will remain with us in spirit. We have mementos from days gone by, and we have sweet memories to hold on to. They will not be forgotten. The legacies left by each of them were so pleasing to God.

Hopefully, those legacies will still impact others for years to come. God used them for His good. They served Him well, and He was able to extend His goodness to others through their good works for Him.

People need God. God doesn't need us to bless others, but He chooses to use us for His purposes. Lindsi was willing to be used. Wanda was willing to do work for God in her life as well. May the same be said of me in my life and the lives of my sons.

Lindsi's life was a blessing to behold. It was amazing to witness her love for God in her life. Her life was a testimony, and it told the story of the close relationship that each of us can have with God. She was a light for Him. She was the salt that God desires for us to be. Her thoughts, actions, and deeds glorified God. Again, Lindsi was one of the many blessings that I have received in my life. She brightened my life, her mother's life, and her brothers' lives. In her shortened life, she accomplished so many things for God through her willingness to be available to be used for His plans. Her thoughtfulness and kindness toward others indicated her love for her Savior. Lindsi's servanthood magnified the goodness that she possessed, and the sincerity in her actions reflected her desire to serve God. Her actions were not showy but genuine, and her good deeds were not the reason for her salvation. Her salvation came through her faith in God. She now enjoys that salvation in a place of beauty beyond human comprehension.

We cannot fathom how beautiful or magnificent it will be. I can't imagine the splendor of the streets of gold or the mansions He created in Heaven for us as believers. Lindsi and Wanda are now there, shouting praises to God and worshipping Him. How awesome just to think about Heaven but also to be a resident there forever.

God has a place for those who have accepted Him in faith. Lindsi had that faith as a child. I wonder if children become adults in their new bodies there. Will our bodies even look like that of our earthly bodies? Well, we won't know until we get there. Thoughts of Heaven give me joy, and believing in the salvation of Lindsi and Wanda through the grace of God brings me peace. This peace that resides within me only comes from my faith in God. I need His comfort in my life each day, and this only comes from Him. If you don't know God, and you want the joy, peace, and comfort that I speak of, confess that you are a sinner in need of a savior, and then confess Jesus as your Lord and Savior.

I want to say, one more time, how honored and blessed I was to be Lindsi's father. She was a daughter that any father would be proud of. It has also been an honor to write her story from my perspective as her father. She was a normal young girl who lived an extraordinary life for God. Her example made an impact for Him. Hers was a life that was surrendered to God. She was committed to showing God's love by showing her love and concern for others, and she was willing to be a servant for Him. She thought about others before she thought of herself. This was evident in her life as she showed compassion. Again, her actions were led by her love for God. She had a genuine faith and showed it outwardly. Her life was a life well spent, and I believe it was also a life that greatly pleased God.

As I close, I want to acknowledge, once again, my thankfulness to God for His blessings and presence in our journey and for lifting us up and carrying us through our trials. I thank God for His faithfulness and His goodness. I also want to thank Him for His calling to write Lindsi's story and to share her testimony and mine as well.

Our family has experienced long journeys of loss. It has been another distant journey to get this book completed. I have talked about Lindsi to others for a long time, but I wanted to tell her story to a broader audience through this book, but I also felt God's leading to tell it as well. I pray that each one who reads this book will experience the innumerable blessings that our family has received from our gracious God and that you will share those testimonies of blessings with others.

We, as believers, should have stories to tell of the greatness of God. Lindsi's story is just one of many. I'm thankful that I could share her story. It's important to note that I had more than one goal in writing this book, other than just telling you about Lindsi's life. I wanted people to see her relationship with God and how she maintained that relationship, even through her suffering, and to reveal her love and faith in God.

Another purpose of mine was to share stories of the many blessings that God provided for us and to acknowledge His goodness. I wanted to expose and make known the power and sovereignty He displayed in our journey and the mercy and grace He granted to us. Plus, I wanted to tell others of His presence that was visually manifested before my very eyes and to attest to the comfort and peace He gave to each of us.

In addition, I also wanted to give recognition to God's movement in my life to pursue this undertaking. There is one last goal, and this one is the most important. The ultimate goal was and is for this book to touch the lives of others and to bring glory and honor to God. This endeavor has been a long quest, and the sadness, pain, and grief reappeared to me during the writing process, but God made a way for me to work through all of those emotions and keep my focus on His will and plan.

The road to writing has been a long and winding one filled with roadblocks. There were both attractions and distractions along the way. The attractions involved my responsibilities as a parent and father because those were the important things that needed my attention. Family time spent together and parenting took precedence over the writing, but I prayed that this book would be published eventually if God so ordained even though it looked like it might never come to fruition. The distractions came when I allowed those things that were not important to grab hold of me. Early in 2024, I felt God calling me to conclude my manuscript. He provided a period of time for me to fully focus my efforts toward its completion, and after ten long years, the story of Lindsi's life had been written. Praise God!

God has been with me every step of the way, just as He was always with my family during our times of trials and grief, but through all of the pain and sorrow, His blessings abounded and His love overflowed. I greatly miss my daughter and my wife as my sons do but, our losses are now Heaven's gains. Lindsi and Wanda now enjoy life eternally. I thank God for calling me to this venture, and I am also honored to be given this opportunity to share Lindsi's incredible story with the world.

Lindsi's life was a testimony, and her legacy keeps that testimony alive today.

Author Biography

Tim Fancher never envisioned himself as an author, even though he earned a degree in History and had gained some writing experience along the way. But, later circumstances in life opened his eyes to becoming a writer.

After graduating from high school, Tim received a college scholarship to play baseball at Mississippi College. After his sophomore year at MC, he transferred to Mississippi State University, where he played college baseball and won the 1989 SEC regular-season championship as a pitcher. Then, he graduated with honors from Mississippi State University and served at his alma mater as an award-winning Academic Advisor (Coordinator) to undeclared and pre-engineering students. In 2013, he was named Staff Advisor of the Year and received a NACADA (National Academic Advising Association) Certificate of Merit for outstanding advising.

Tim has always been a family man—he and his wife Wanda had three children: Lindsi, Logan, and Larson, the apples of their parents' eyes. But when Lindsi was diagnosed with a rare brain tumor, life changed for the Fancher family. After Lindsi's death, Tim felt called by God to share his family's story— the duplicity of horrifying grief and inspiring courage. *Lindsi's*

Legacy is Tim's first book, a mission to share hope when all seems lost.

Tim is now retired, and as a Christian, he is passionate about sharing Lindsi's story because it also allows him the opportunity to share his testimony of God's grace for him and his family. In all things, Tim desires to bring honor to the Lord through proclaiming the truth of God's mercy and love. In his spare time, Tim works on his various hobby collections—from baseball cards to coins and other interesting sundries.

Tim's life has been riddled with loss—first when his daughter succumbed to cancer and later, when his wife died of COVID-19, but through it all, his faith in God has never wavered. Through his pain, Tim reflects on one of his favorite Bible verses, Ephesians 6:10. "Finally, be strong in the Lord and in the strength of his might." This verse reminds him of God's ever- present strength that has carried him through life's obstacles.

Milton Keynes UK
Ingram Content Group UK Ltd.
UKHW021133040824
446423UK00008B/16

9 798218 462031